Exploring MUSEUMS

Scotland

Half title page

Detail from an illuminated initial in the Arbuthnot Missal (ill. p. 77). Paisley Museum and Art Gallery, Paisley.

Front Cover

Clockwise: Wemyss Ware cat made by Robert Heron & Son, Fife Pottery, Kirkcaldy, c.1900 – Kirkcaldy Museum and Art Gallery, Kirkcaldy; 'Admiral' shop sign acquired from David Stalkes, Nautical Opticians, Leith – Huntly House Museum, Edinburgh; 3-cylinder Rolls-Royce, 1905 – Doune Motor Museum, Doune (on loan from Royal Scottish Automobile Club); Hawick from Wilton Lodge by J.B. Pringle, 1850 – Hawick Museum and The Scott Gallery, Hawick; Brass Highland ring brooch, 17th century, from Tomintoul, Banffshire – Royal Museum of Scotland, Queen Street, Edinburgh; Hunter's microscope, with items from his various collections – Hunterian Museum, Glasgow; In the Car by Roy Lichtenstein (b.1923) – Scottish National Gallery of Modern Art, Edinburgh; Ten-gallon punchbowl given to the seven trades of Dumfries to commemorate the opening of the Trades Hall in 1806 – Dumfries Museum and Camera Obscura, Dumfries; A Glasgow shopkeeper of the 1790s by an unknown artist – People's Palace Museum, Glasgow.
Centre: Chanter, mouthpiece and part of drone of Kinlochmoidart pipes played at Bannockburn (1314), the bag covered with the ancient Clanranald tartan – The Clan Donald Centre (Museum of the Isles), Armadale, Isle of Skye.

MUSEUMS & GALLERIES COMMISSION

A MUSEUMS ASSOCIATION GUIDE

Exploring MUSEUMS

Scotland

Colin Thompson

LONDON: HMSO

© Crown Copyright 1990
First published 1990
ISBN 0 11 290474 2

British Library Cataloguing in
Publication Data
A CIP catalogue record for this book is
available from the British Library

HMSO publications are available from:

HMSO Publications Centre
(Mail and telephone orders only)
PO Box 276, London, SW8 5DT
Telephone orders 071–873 9090
General enquiries 071–873 0011
(queuing system in operation for both numbers)

HMSO Bookshops
49 High Holborn, London, WC1V 6HB 071–873 0011 (Counter service only)
258 Broad Street, Birmingham, B1 2HE 021–643 3740
Southey House, 33 Wine Street, Bristol, BS1 2BQ (0272) 264306
9–21 Princess Street, Manchester, M60 8AS 061–834 7201
80 Chichester Street, Belfast, BT1 4JY (0232) 238451
71 Lothian Road, Edinburgh, EH3 9AZ 031–228 4181

HMSO's Accredited Agents
(see Yellow Pages)

and through good booksellers

CONTENTS

FOREWORD

President of the Museums Association
Patrick Boylan
and the Chairman of the Museums & Galleries Commission
Brian Morris

The first volumes of *Exploring Museums* were published in Museums Year, which marked the centenary of the Museums Association. When the Association's first conference was held in York in 1889, there were already several hundred museums in Britain. Now there are some 2,300, and new ones are opening every month. They vary enormously in size and scope, from the large all-purpose museum to the small collection in a converted house. Many of the smaller museums are less well known than they should be, and it is these particularly that the books in this series seek to highlight.

Never before have museums in general been as popular as they are today. In 1989 alone they received between them something like 100 million visits (which is more than any sport or other leisure activity). They are especially attractive to young people, to the curious of all ages and to the lovers of beautiful, unusual and exciting things. There are indeed museums for every taste and interest, for every day and in every area. We are sure that these books will help many more people to discover the museums of the British Isles, to learn from them and to enjoy them.

BUCKINGHAM PALACE

As Patron of Museums Year 1989, I hope that through this series
of Regional Guides "Exploring Museums", you will derive great enjoyment
from the fascinating world of museums and galleries; there are some
two thousand of them offering an immense variety and range of experiences
so there is something for everyone. It is so exciting to feel the
sense of exploring new areas in the world of museums and galleries.
Make the most of what is on offer in 1989.

Sarah.

January 1989

EDITOR'S NOTE

This volume is one of a series of eleven regional guides to museums in the British Isles. The term 'museum' is often applied to a wide variety of collections and buildings: most of the places selected for description in the *Exploring Museums* guides, however, comply as far as possible with the Museums Association's definition of a museum as 'an institution that collects, documents, preserves, exhibits and interprets material evidence and associated information for the public benefit'.

Given the sheer quantity of museums in the British Isles, the guides describe only a selection, concentrating on those places that authors considered most worthy of a visit, either because of the quality of their collections and displays, or because of the interesting or unusual nature of what they have on view. Museums in each area not described in full are listed at the back of the guides, with brief details of their collections; please note that some of these are only open by appointment. The lists include new museums that are scheduled to open in the near future.

The principal aim of this series is to describe, through words and pictures, the types of things that visitors can expect to see and do at various museums. Authors have tried to put themselves in the shoes of a general museum visitor, and present a personal rather than an official view in their descriptions. It should be noted that specific items they describe may not be on show when you visit: most museums now change their displays fairly often, and if you want to see something in particular you should check beforehand with the museum concerned. Most of the illustrations have been selected by the authors, and highlight lesser-known objects and museum activities, as well as exhibits for which particular museums are renowned. Basic information about access and facilities has been kept to a minimum, as opening times or bus routes, for example, are frequently subject to change; please check with museums before visiting for precise details of opening times, holiday closures, admission prices, and how to get there, and for information on special events and activities.

Krystyna Matyjaszkiewicz
Series Editor

The views expressed in this guide are those of the author and not necessarily those of the Museums Association.

As the Scottish Museums Council was closely involved in the original discussions which resulted in the commissioning of the series, it is particularly pleasing to be able to welcome the Scottish volume.

One of Britain's first collections was founded in Scotland nearly 400 years ago. Now you may study European prehistory, the limits of Rome's empire, and the Scots' central part in Britain's civil, military and imperialist past. The work of world pioneer anthropologists, entomologists, engineers, photographers and explorers may be scanned where they were born, together with past and present innovations in the investigation of fossils, earth and space science, whaling, oil and medicine. There are native works of art whose virtue foreign connoisseurs have belatedly recognised as worthy to place beside more famous contemporaries.

So if you visit our museums and galleries with an open mind, they will open that mind further, to a realisation that this small outlier on the far north-eastern fringe of Europe has been a home of ideas and activities without which mankind would have been poorer.

The wealth and variety of our collections are by no means confined to the major museums and galleries in Edinburgh and Glasgow, and this volume's distinguished author (himself one of our most scholarly curators) will set you on your path of exploration.

Trevor Clark, Chairman, Scottish Museums Council

INTRODUCTION

What is distinctive about Scotland's museums springs from what is distinctive about the Scots – resourceful, questioning, imaginative – and about the land they inhabit, much of it stony, difficult of access and with an apparently endless seaboard. The livelihood of the people was at first in crofting and the fisheries, and later in heavy industry with coal and steel. It's a story of physical hardship with flashes of poetry from the life of the imagination and from a strong community spirit, which we glimpse as much in the life of the crofter on Lewis as in the workers' meetings on Glasgow Green, beside the **People's Palace**.

Scotland's museum tradition was established by independent people in the smaller towns from Kelso to Elgin, who formed themselves in the early part of last century into Philosophical Societies ('philosophy' was then applied to any kind of scientific enquiry). The study of the land, its stones, fossils and prehistoric remains, bred James Hutton and Hugh Miller and other pioneers of geology and archaeology. The problem of communication bred Thomas Telford. Industrial engineering bred James Watt and Lord Kelvin. Meanwhile tourism, following in the path of the royal household to Balmoral, provided the impetus for a number of photographers in Grampian and the north in the pioneering days of the 1850s.

Sometimes, as if in opposition to the Presbyterian devotion to the literal word and the scientific fact, Scotland's legends seem as important to her imaginative life as her history, perhaps more so. Legend and history intertwine – as the visitor to museums in Ayrshire or the north west discovers – in Robert Burns and the Bonnie Prince.

It was a part of Scotland's strong sea-faring tradition that seamen from towns on her long coastline would bring back curiosities from distant parts: a giant tortoise from the Seychelles, a shrunken head from Borneo, a mummified princess from Peru. Some of these things have been allowed to survive – in **Greenock, Elgin, Nairn, Peterhead, Perth** and elsewhere. Others (not only in Scotland) succumbed to the blinkered inter-war doctrine that 'local' museums should show only what was native or natural to their own area. If you weren't brought up in a big city, what went on in the wide world outside was not supposed to be your business. So a number of our local ethnography collections were sold, burnt or brought into Edinburgh or Glasgow.

Several collectors stand out: for example Dr Isobel Grant, the pioneer of folk museums in Britain, and two vastly divergent personalities, both of international standing, William Hunter and William Burrell. Hunter was a doctor and polymath of the 18th century, whose extraordinary collection ranged from scientific evidence to a powerful Rembrandt sketch. Burrell, an eccentric shipowner of our own century, collected things on a grand scale for their beauty or their antiquity, attributes that are sometimes hard to distinguish.

Among historic houses I have singled out only **Dunrobin**, whose museum is being restored as a rare and precious survival of an earlier concept of the museum. Paradoxically, the idea of a place where nothing is ever changed has now been transferred from the museum to historic houses and National Trust properties, where we tend to expect everything to be kept just as it was. Meanwhile, our museums are in continuous change. This poses difficulties in producing a guide of this kind, for by the time it is published new museums will have opened in Scotland and, even more important, others will have changed their displays to match today's expectations.

Of the 230 or so museums that qualified for inclusion, there was room for less than a third to be described at any length. In making the choice, I had in mind the enquiring tourist – people travelling to unfamiliar places with sufficient curiosity to want to discover something about their character and history, and the special things that can be seen there. So I have left out those museums, however excellent, that cater mainly for people living nearby or for people with a specialised interest in a particular subject. At the same time I have tried to convey some of my delight at coming upon small museums in out-of-the-way places that proved to be unexpectedly rewarding. The museums at **Ruthwell, Wanlockhead, Meigle, Gairloch, Golspie, Creetown**, and the **Pier Arts Centre, Stromness** have neither subject matter nor its treatment in common, but they share the precious power of capturing our imagination.

At least of capturing my imagination, for museum-going is a subjective business. I personally respond more readily to the products of man than of nature, especially those made less than 2,000 years ago, and I tend to see the interest of the regimental museum as a rather specialised one. The difficulty is that a multitude of specialised interests is what museums are about. But whereas museums were once seen as places where the specialist could supplement the knowledge he had already gained from books, they are now valued for the insights they can offer into subjects that are new to us (including the history of places we visit for the first time): they have become the *hors-d'oeuvre* rather than the dessert.

The much wider museum-going public of the last two or three decades has brought with it the challenge to curators of holding the interest of people in widely varying states of knowledge. In subjects I know nothing about, I prefer to be shown a few significant items and to be told their story – for instance the formation and mining of coal. If I already knew all about that, I might be more interested in samples of the different types of coal.

Would you rather see a collection of 1,000 coins and pick out the ones that interest you, or be shown only the most unusual or distinctive of them, and be told why? And if you think it is impossible for a museum to satisfy both these preferences, have a look at the coin display in the **Hunterian Museum, Glasgow**. The old system and the new were (until 1989) side by side in the two natural history displays of **Perth Museum**, and the two approaches are typified at their best by the ethnographic displays at **Glasgow Art Gallery & Museum** and the **Aberdeen Anthropological Museum**.

The tourist who visits more than one or two social history or folk museums encounters a different aspect of this dilemma. For the specialist, there are significant variations between the crofting houses on Lewis, Orkney and Skye, although for other people their salient characteristics are common to them all. Conversely, Scottish silver, Victorian domestic equipment or the apparatus of the fishing and coopering industries are very properly found in a number of our museums; it is no use to a schoolboy in Kirkcudbright to know that he could see them if only he had been born in Peterhead. In this guide I have tried to focus on what is distinctive to each place and to each museum.

The shortcoming of any guide is in what it leaves out. There is so much more to our museums than what the visitor is able to see at any one time. For one thing, collections are usually far more extensive than what is on display (things like watercolours and textiles are damaged anyway by long exposure to the light). Besides this, most curators are experts in their field and have a wide knowledge of their district. In nearly all museums there is provision for my enquiring tourists to discover more – but they have to ask.

Colin Thompson   January 1989

ACKNOWLEDGEMENTS

The Museums Association is grateful to the museums described for generously lending photographs and agreeing to their reproduction herein.

Further acknowledgement is due to the following:

Cover, 1790s painting of a shopkeeper, Colour plates 6 and 7, and illustrations pp. 49–51 (Burrell Collection, Glasgow Art Gallery & Museum) and 54–56 (Museum of Transport, People's Palace Museum) © Glasgow Museums and Art Galleries; Cover, Roy Lichtenstein, Colour plate 9, and illustrations pp. 32–33 (National Gallery of Scotland) and 37–40 (Scottish National Gallery of Modern Art, Scottish National Portrait Gallery) © Trustees of the National Galleries of Scotland; Colour plate 9, photo. Antonia Reeve; Cover, Highland ring brooch, Colour plate 10, and illustrations pp. 34–37 (Royal Museum of Scotland, Chambers Street, and Queen Street), 41 (Scottish United Services Museum) and 74–75 (Shambellie House Museum of Costume) © Trustees of the National Museums of Scotland; p. 27, top, photo. Ron Gazzard, Dundee; p. 28, bottom, Crown Copyright; pp. 69–70 (Meigle) and p. 90 (Arnol) photographs courtesy of Scottish Development Department, Crown Copyright; p. 91 (Corrigall), photo. Gunnie Muberg; p. 95 (Pier Arts Centre), photo. Richard Welsby; p. 95 (Stromness Museum), photo. William Hourston.

Special photography by Mark Thompson: Cover, Kinlochmoidart pipes; Colour plate 11 (Gairloch); illustrations pp. 7–8 (Burns Cottage & Museum), p. 12 (Auchindrain), p. 24 (Dunbeath), p. 28 (Easdale Island), p. 42 (Elgin), pp. 43–44 (Eyemouth), p. 45 (West Highland Museum, exterior), pp. 47–48 (Gairloch), pp. 57–58 (Golspie), pp. 68–69 (Kirkcudbright), pp. 73–74 (Nairn), p. 76 (Newtongrange), p. 86 (Tain), pp. 88–89 (Wick), pp. 98–100 (Isle of Skye).

Key to Symbols Used

(B) Borders Region; (C) Central Region; (D) Dumfries and Galloway Region; (F) Fife Region; (G) Grampian Region; (H) Highland Region; (L) Lothian Region; (O) Orkney, Shetland, Western Isles; (S) Strathclyde Region; (T) Tayside Region. See regional maps.

F Free admission

§ Admission charge

V Voluntary donation requested

◫ Restaurant/cafeteria on premises

P Car Park on premises

⯆ Good access and facilities for disabled

♿ Difficult/limited access and facilities for disabled and infirm

   W Unstepped access via main or side door, wheelchair spaces, and adapted toilet

   T Adapted toilet

   X Flat or one-step access

   A Access with 2–5 steps, or split level exhibition space

   S Many unavoidable steps and/or other obstacles for wheelchair users and the infirm

   G Provision made for guide dogs

   (based on disabled access code devised by ARTSLINE (071 388 2227), the free telephone information service on the arts in Greater London for people with disabilities)

⚏ Group visits

⚏ School group visits

☺ Workshops/holiday events/guided tours/talks – 'phone for details

Museums shown in **bold** type in the text are described in full elsewhere in the volume; those shown in *italic* type are briefly described in the list of museums and collections at the back.

ABERDEEN (G)

Aberdeen Art Gallery

Schoolhill, Aberdeen AB9 1FQ
(0224) 646333
Open daily. 🇫 ▣ ♿ ☺

John Lavery, The Tennis Party, *1885*

The Gallery was built in 1885, but what we now see dates substantially from 1905, when the main hall and exterior were built. This great central hall has a colonnade surrounding it with columns made of different kinds of granite, the stone for which Aberdeen is famous. The large central space is surmounted by a great flat oval roof-light, and a balcony at first floor level. It is a kind of apotheosis of the old museum design that can still be seen at **Forres, Elgin** and **Montrose**, and in a rather more provincial form at **Kirkcudbright**. In the centre there is now a fountain that plays across a sculpture by Barbara Hepworth, a fitting symbol for the Gallery's dedication to contemporary art and the imagination with which it is treated.

The hall is a good place for displaying contemporary pieces of sculpture, since the layout encourages their display with substantial spaces in between them. There is also plenty of room for paintings: in one part of the entrance area there were, for example, in 1988, large paintings by Bridget Riley, Bert Irvin, and Gilbert and George, but no doubt they have been, or soon will be, deposed and new, challenging works will come to take their place.

Contemporary art, with a strong bias towards British and particularly Scottish artists, has been the key to the Gallery's collection through its association with Alexander MacDonald. MacDonald made his money in the granite industry, inheriting his father's business in 1860. By the 1870s, partly paralysed and confined to a wheelchair, he was busily engaged in buying the work of contemporary artists and getting to know the artists themselves in the process, a factor that he considered very important to his understanding of art. MacDonald died in 1884 and left his collection to the

Sir Stanley Spencer, Southwold, *1937*

Gallery. The MacDonald Room contains a rich range of 19th century paintings, the atmosphere set by plants in the centre. Notable are 'The Tennis Party' by Lavery, and works by three Aberdonians – Farquharson's 'Afterglow', small landscapes by Dyce, and John Phillip's 'Baptism in Scotland' of 1850.

Earlier paintings on show are mainly British, including notably Wilkie's 'Wellington writing despatches' and an 18th century portrait group by Zoffany. There is a group of Impressionists, including Sisley, Monet and Renoir, and a room is reserved for drawings and watercolours of all periods, again mainly British, from Blake and Rowlandson to James Cowie and Jack

Knox. The balcony above the main hall is used to display contemporary prints.

Besides leaving his collection to the gallery, MacDonald left a substantial endowment for the purchase of further pictures. With a modesty and foresight that are not too common, he imposed the condition that 'no pictures painted more than 25 years before the date of purchase shall be eligible.' Since his bequest, successive directors have kept well to its spirit, and it is worth watching the dates at which some of the works were acquired: Zadkine in 1953, Fernand Leger in 1937, Henry Moore in the 1950s, and the captivating vision of Southwold beach by Stanley Spencer in 1938, for example.

One result is that the room of British

Interior view, Aberdeen Art Gallery

Aberdeen Maritime Museum

Provost Ross's House, Shiprow,
Aberdeen AB1 2BY   (0224) 585788
Closed Sundays. 🅵 ♿

The first thing about Aberdeen Maritime Museum is the building it's in, the subject of a recent rescue operation. Provost Ross's house is the city's oldest surviving building, dating from 1594 (it is actually two houses that were joined together). Seen from the street, it is very attractive to modern eyes with its numerous small windows and with the original main door set into an arcaded recess. The building was derelict when it was rescued in 1954 by the National Trust for Scotland, who now lease it to Aberdeen City Council for use as the Maritime Museum, which was opened in 1984.

Provost Ross was a merchant of the 18th century with substantial shipping interests, and his house is on the cobbled street Shiprow, which was at one time the only access road to the upper harbour. (One of the museum windows looks out onto the upper harbour, and there is a note beside it giving the names of the vessels that are currently berthed.) A very good illustrated booklet on the museum includes notes on the house and on the history of the harbour itself as well as other aspects of the museum collections.

Only fragmentary impressions of the original building can be detected in-

art ranges from Spencer, Ivon Hitchens, Augustus John, Victor Pasmore and Matthew Smith to Robin Philipson, Elizabeth Blackadder and the distinguished Aberdonian James Cowie, a painter's painter. Some of these are now history, and the display gives a remarkably comprehensive view of the period from the 1920s to the present day. Here and there discreet notes on individual pictures draw the visitor's attention to their particular visual virtues.

At the back of the main hall is an area devoted to crafts. There is a strong representation of Chinese ceramics, lacquer and cloisonné enamels, which were given by Dr James Cromar Watt, an Aberdeen architect who was collecting in the first half of this century. The main displays of British pottery and ceramics go back to the 1930s, but there are also earlier examples from Wedgwood. These are all shown with dignity and distinction in free-standing showcases.

The present Director is a practising painter of considerable standing, and in the Gallery's policy now there is no mistaking the dedication to the art of the present, and to the art that is being produced in Scotland especially.

A sense of liveliness here is not entirely due to the presence of contemporary works of art. Apart from the main displays, there is a very active programme of temporary exhibitions, a link with the Peacock Printmakers' Workshop in Aberdeen, and provision for a resident craftsman for three months of the year and a resident artist for another six months. Besides this, the gallery is seldom without schoolchildren, the large spaces encouraging them to run about.

On one side of the hall, opposite to the cafeteria, is a large and extremely well stocked bookshop. Recent publications include an excellent picture book of the Gallery's paintings and an illustrated account of Aberdeen Archaeology.

Provost Ross's house

side: occasional low doorways, old stairs, changes of floor level and one or two rooms of 18th century date. One of these is given up to a reconstruction of the office of the Duthie family, who were both shipowners and shipbuilders in the 19th century.

There is a wide range of ship models, for example a very picturesque large model of the 'Schip' of 1689, rigged as a fifth-rate warship, and a model of the first purpose-built clipper, the 'Stornoway', built at Aberdeen in 1850 for Jardine Matheson to carry tea from China. There are half-models used by shipbuilders in the course of construction, models made of their ship by the captain or a member of the crew, a small fleet of different kinds of herring fishing craft, and even a ship in a bottle. There are paintings of boats, too, one of the most distinguished being of a Scottish warship of about 1590, probably by a Dutch painter.

Displays on the seagoing trades reflect the fact that Aberdeen was at one time Scotland's biggest whaling port, active between the mid-18th and mid-19th centuries, and her busiest herring fishing port (a distinction that has now been surrendered to Peterhead). A room is devoted to the herring fishing industry, illustrated by old photographs, and with costumed figures filling herring barrels and carrying creels (fish baskets).

There are clear descriptions of Aberdeen harbour, which was substantially man-made, since it necessitated considerable dredging and widening. It was a going concern by the beginning of the 18th century, and remains important to this day. The section ends with a model of the roll-on, roll-off vehicle ferries (or 'Ro-Ro' ferries).

Up another little stairway we see a tableau of a team of ship's riveters. And finally, at the top of the house, is a room devoted to an explanation of the oil industry. Much of the space is taken up with a very large and magnificently detailed scale model of a rig, and a short audio-visual programme gives the background. There is a fascinating incongruity between this display of the 1980s and the building of 1594 that houses it.

Model of the 'Schip', 1689

Model of an oil rig

Anthropological Museum

*University of Aberdeen, Marischal
College, Broad Street, Aberdeen
AB9 1AS   (0224) 273131*
Closed Saturdays. **F**
&: access is by a double flight of
stairs.
m & **m** welcome but must book in
advance.

Whereas the Victorian museum was
built at the top of a flight of steps,
which advertised it proudly and intimi-
dated unruly little boys as they climbed
up to it, the traditional university pre-
cinct is an enclave specially designed to
keep the ignorant masses out. This
makes it extremely difficult for university museums, in Aberdeen as elsewhere, to bring people in, now that
they are keen to attract as wide a public
as possible.

But the visitor who penetrates the
university court of Marischal College is
rewarded by an eye-opening, provoca-
tive introduction to the study of man.
This is the main display in the Anthropological Museum, newly created in
1985, which is addressed to those of us
who have no specialised knowledge of
the subject.

It is housed in one of the museum's
two large rooms, which has been given
a mezzanine floor to allow more display
space. Metal stair and supports to the
mezzanine are painted in a strong red,
a colour motif that runs through the
exhibition area. The second room is to
be preserved in its original Victorian
Gothic of 1846, top-lit with an elegant
wooden stair at the far end leading to a
gallery that goes right round. Plans are
in hand to use it for the display of the
social history of the north east of Scotland.

The present display is entitled 'A
museum about human beings – about
being human', and we quickly discover
that our own curious and wayward
tribal customs are under review just as
much as the behaviour of the native
tribes or 'savages' from the past. The
first exhibit is a pillar with caricatures

Wood statuette, Yoruba people, Nigeria

of Aberdonians, and the next is two
life-sized figures of a bush man and
woman, made in 1880, with a notice
hanging from them on which they pro-
test at being treated as exhibits in a
museum.

The tone is set, and whatever rituals
and customs are shown from other
societies, there will be constant com-

parisons with our own. A modern high-
heeled shoe is shown beside the shoes
used to deform the feet of Chinese
women. The extraordinary costume of
netted fibre worn by young men after
their initiation at puberty in Angola is
shown beside a description and photograph of the initiation of stable hands
in Angus in the 1920s.

The display is divided into themes:
man as toolmaker, warrior, hunter –
woman as provider; witches and wise
women; great mother, magic and
medicine. Sometimes the titles are
more aggressively up to date: 'Old men
rule O.K.', or 'Does the Queen wear

Scribe, Egyptian statuette

Part of 'The Living Dead' display

ALFORD (G)

Grampian Transport Museum & Railway Museum

Alford, Aberdeenshire AB3 8AD
(09755) 62292
Closed mid-October to March. ⬛
🅿 ♿
⛹ & ⛹ welcome but must book in advance. ◎

The fact that the village of Alford exists at all is because it was the place chosen for the terminus of the Great North Scotland Railway in 1859. Then, over a century later, the decision was taken to develop the village as a centre for leisure and tourism. When the need was felt for a museum concerned expressly with the history of transport in north-east Scotland, Alford was seen as the natural location for it. By 1982 sufficient funds had been realised, with the co-operation of the Regional Council and the EEC, to build a large new exhibition hall for the road transport display and to rebuild the railway terminus. The exhibition hall was opened in 1983 and the railway station the following spring.

her crown in bed, Mummy?' for a display of official robes. Occasionally they are more acid, like 'With God on our side'.

The risk to which thematic displays of this kind are prone, of assaulting the visitor with congealed masses of text, is mostly overcome. There is no doubt about the underlying scholarship and the conviction that springs from it, but it is not often that the commentary becomes so long, so learned or so abstract as to leave the layman behind. The text is mostly restricted to hints – often by quoting statements made by anyone from expert anthropologists to Marshall McLuhan and Raymond Chandler – and to minimal descriptions of the objects.

In the end the objects themselves are the element on which the value of the exhibition relies. These have been drawn from the ethnographical collection of the University, which is of remarkable range and distinction. The basis of it was the work of Dr Robert Wilson, who was educated at Marischal College and spent the years 1819–22 travelling and studying in Europe and Asia, and later left his collection to the University. In his journals he describes the discovery and acquisition – not always under what would now be considered ethical circumstances – of many of his prizes.

Among them are many things remarkable for their inventiveness or state of preservation, or for the beauty of their craftsmanship: an eskimo carving in soapstone; a shrine carving in three storeys from 19th century Yoruba; an 18th century Buddhist guardian lion in porcelain; an outrigger canoe for shark fishing, carved with extreme elegance from the breadfruit tree in Papua New Guinea; a basketry head with dogs' teeth from the Hawaiian Islands; a Tibetan prayer wheel enclosed in a decorated wooden chest; an extraordinary elongated image of a human head, carved from tree fern in Vanatu, Malekula Islands; or the lid in high relief of the mummy of an Egyptian 5-year old girl. It is a long list.

With objects of such distinction, the risk is that they are shown merely as examples, their individual character being ignored. But it is one of the achievements of this display that each individual object is accorded its due dignity, things produced as works of art being presented as works of art. This is achieved by the sympathy with which the objects themselves, and the human cultures that gave rise to them, have been understood.

Arrol Johnston dog cart, 1902

The Craigievar Express

Unlike the museum at **Doune**, which displays a fairly small group of aristocrats of the road, most of them with individual pedigrees, the Alford museum aims to represent the whole history of road transport, so that the visitor can follow how motor vehicles have been developed, and more particularly the effect that the internal combustion engine has had on Grampian Region's social and economic history. Backing up the displays is the museum's booklet, 'An introduction to Grampian's road transport history'.

One of the curiosities of the collection is the 'Craigievar Express', a strange three-wheeled steam-driven vehicle designed and built by the postman at Craigievar, four miles to the south of Alford, and used on his rounds there from 1895, before the arrival of the internal combustion engine.

A fairly dominant feature of the museum is the Mortier Dance Organ. Made in Belgium in 1923, and of a type still to be seen and heard in the streets of Brussels, it has over 400 pipes and a full set of drums, and a façade in a flamboyant 'art deco' style. When it plays, its uproarious fairground music fills the museum hall. It has to be said that its claim to a Grampian connection is tenuous, and its limited mobility makes its status in the history of transport at all

rather questionable. But like the nickelodeon in Edinburgh's **Museum of Childhood**, its best justification may be that it regularly sets the visitors' feet tapping.

Other unusual exhibits include a traction engine, an Arrol Johnston dog cart of 1902, and a portable steam engine (which did not move under its own steam) presented by the Duke of Edinburgh from the Balmoral Estate. In 1988 this was awaiting restoration to working condition.

There are altogether around 100 vehicles on display at any one time, including bicycles, motorcycles, veteran, vintage and classic cars, steam vehicles, fire engines, agricultural vehicles, lorries, horse-drawn carriages,

and a tram from Aberdeen. The greater part of what the visitor will see in the museum is likely to be on loan from private owners in Scotland. Vehicles are acquired for the permanent collection only occasionally; to qualify they must normally be of practical use or of exceptional interest and importance to the region.

There is a reconstruction of an early garage of the type that was common in Scotland after the 1914–18 war. (Garages in country districts were usually developed by enterprising blacksmiths who had the foresight to diversify their trade.) There is also a wheelwright's shop, which is accompanied by a short video showing the craft of making wooden wheels.

The museum is complemented by a display on the history of the old Great North of Scotland Railway at the Alford Valley Railway Museum. This is housed in the village station of Alford nearby, which is the terminus of the Alford Valley Railway, Scotland's only 2ft gauge passenger railway. The two venues act as a focus for transport enthusiasts, and local interest and enthusiasm for rail and road transport are kept alive with rallies, steam-up days and other events.

[Latest additions to the museum include a children's adventure playground, situated just outside; a Grampian Transport double-decker bus, with video displays on road transport and motorsport; and a 1966 driving simulator, which allows visitors to have a shot at 'driving'. Ed.]

General view of the transport display

ALLOWAY (S)

Burns Cottage & Museum

Alloway, Ayr KA7 4PY
(0282) 41215
Closed Sundays in winter.
🔋 (includes admission to *Burns Monument*). ▣ ♿

Although birthplaces of the famous have generally been excluded from this guide, the cottage at Alloway has to be an exception. The 'clay biggin' is the oldest building in the village, built in 1758 by Burns' father William, who was a market gardener. It must already have been a place of pilgrimage as the birthplace of Robert Burns when an engraving of it was published in 1801, by which time it was in use as an alehouse. The cottage was restored in 1899, and it was no doubt at this time that the adjoining land was laid out as a park for the visitors, with a group of four yew trees now grown large and venerable.

There is no attempt to evoke the smell or the untidiness of the past. The cottage is neatly thatched, and whitewashed throughout. It is clean and well tended, and we have a proper sense of making a pilgrimage to a shrine. We walk through the building on its stone flagged floors; first the byre for the animals, with bare rafters in the roof, then a room that now houses Burns' desk, the box bed where he was born, and the living room with its press and dresser. A touching reminder of the long history of the shrine are the Victorian brass plaques screwed to the chairs, declaring their association with the poet, a museum practice that has long since fallen out of favour.

Nearby is the museum, which is a recent building. The most important element of its collection is a group of manuscripts, mainly letters and drafts of poems, and also some of Burns' papers as an exciseman. One of the more recent acquisitions is the Gra-

Burns Cottage

ham of Fintry collection of holograph letters, including letters from Burns to his patron Robert Graham of Fintry and his wife, bought in 1980.

The collection is still being added to, and it is distinguished by the care with which only things with a real claim to authenticity are on show. Many objects must have been offered that were piously thought to be associated with the poet, which were either gently re-

fused or have since been relegated to the storeroom. Besides the manuscripts, there are many precious relics and memorabilia, including the Burns family bible (bought in 1904), the famous 1786 'Kilmarnock edition' of his poems and other early editions and illustrations of his works, as well as the poet's watch, the poet's snuff mull, the poet's razor, a cast of the poet's skull, and so on.

Section of graphic presentation of Burns's life

The kitchen, Burns Cottage

Maclaurin Art Gallery & Rozelle House

Rozelle Park, Monument Road, Alloway, Ayr KA7 4NQ
(0292) 45447
Open daily. ⬛   ♿ (T under construction 1989).
♿ & ♿ pre-book only if special facilities required; education facilities to be developed in 1990/91.

Rozelle House belonged to Lt Commander John Hamilton RN, who left the house and its fairly extensive grounds to the Royal Burgh of Ayr in 1968 'for the townspeople for cultural and recreational activities'. It is a plain, dignified 18th century house with white rough-cast walls, their details picked out in brown. The entrance and stairway are bright and welcoming and the stairwell is usually hung with paintings from the Maclaurin Art Collection.

Since 1982 the house has been used mainly for the display of items from the collection of Kyle and Carrick District Council. There is a section devoted to civic affairs, with such things as the burgh seal and bailie's chain of office (the District covers an area up to Troon). There is also a display of militaria associated with the Ayrshire Yeomanry and the Ayrshire Gunners, who were disbanded in 1965, and a

The displays in the main exhibition room have been newly redesigned, and now include lively descriptive panels of the poet's life and the social life of his time. A chronological chart sets him in the context of events and people between 1740 and 1800: Cook's voyages, Watt's steam engine, Wordsworth, Turner, Beethoven, the French Revolution.

There is also a spacious art gallery with illustrations of poems and paintings by Burns' contemporaries. Distinguished is 'Mauchline Fair' by Alexander Carse. At one end of the gallery is a case housing four scenes from *Tam o' Shanter* carved in limewood by Thomas Tweedie in about 1869, notable for their dextrous and naturalistic execution.

The museum deserves high praise for the quality of presentation and the discernment with which material has been chosen for inclusion. Not everyone will welcome the continuous soundtrack, but this has at least the virtue of variety, ranging from Burns songs and poems to piping and full orchestral arrangements.

For devotees of 'the immortal memory', Alloway should be the beginning of the Burns trail, which will lead them up the road to the Burns Monument and on through Ayrshire, Dumfries and Galloway, visiting Mauchline, Irvine, Ellisland Farm and above all Dumfries itself.

Kilmarnock edition of Burns poems, 1786

Viktor Vasarely, Bellatrix bleu, *print*

R. B. Kitaj, Man in a Blue Cloak, *1982*

display of earlier Scottish paintings. [The latter to be phased out during 1989. Ed.]

The Art Gallery, situated in the old stable block, was opened in 1976. It is an inviting area where exhibition space combines attractively with features of the original building. In the courtyard, which forms an integral part of the gallery, there is a bronze reclining woman by Henry Moore, which announces the emphasis on contemporary work in the collecting policy of the Trustees.

The gallery itself mainly shows a lively programme of temporary exhibitions. These have come partly from the South Bank Centre, and partly from other organisers; some are generated by members of the South West Galleries Association, to which the museum belongs.

It is the collection of contemporary art however that is the most important aspect of this museum. Although small and of recent origin, it is distinguished among collections in our smaller museums, and rare enough anywhere in Scotland, for its presentation of a courageous and seriously challenging view of the visual arts of our time. And it is noteworthy that unlike, for exam-

ple, the **Pier Arts Centre** in **Stromness** (the other conspicuous example of this kind), it is supported by a District Council, Kyle and Carrick, who work closely with the Maclaurin Trust. The Maclaurin Art Collection has been built up since 1982 with a substantial sum of money bequeathed by the widow of J.H. Maclaurin in memory of her husband, supplemented by the Local Museums Purchase Fund (the annual government grant available to support purchases by local and independent museums). The emphasis is on Scottish or British artists, and purchases so far have included works

by Ivon Hitchens, Robert MacBryde, William Scott, Roger Hilton and Patrick Heron of the older generation and younger artists like Alan Davie, John Bellany, John Hoyland, Bridget Riley and David Nash.

An internal reconstruction of Rozelle House is planned in order to enlarge the exhibition space available, which is expected to be completed by 1992. [This redevelopment will provide extended display areas, with material from the social and natural history collections on the upper floors and temporary exhibitions based on the art collections on the lower floors. Ed.]

John Bellany, The Fishers, *1972*

ANSTRUTHER (F)

Scottish Fisheries Museum

Harbourhead, Anstruther, Fife
KY10 3AB   (0333) 310628
Open daily. 🚻 📷
♿ S: facilities to be improved over
next 2 years.
👤 & 👥 welcome but must book in
advance.

Anstruther is one of the old Fife herring fishing ports, lying at the heart of the East Neuk fishing villages, like St Monans, where fishing boats are still being built, and Crail, the centre of the local crab and lobster fishing. The museum provides a great deal of information about the Fife fisheries but, as the Scottish Fisheries Museum, it also covers the history of the whole industry in Scotland, which went on all round the coast, from the Dundee whalers and commercial salmon fishing to the boats with the herring lasses who left Scotland every year for a season in Lowestoft and Yarmouth.

For the visitor who is new to the scene the most surprising aspect of the industry was its sheer size and the number of people involved. Old photographs of the harbour, taken at times when all the boats were in, show nothing but a dense forest of masts, and there were up to ten jobs ashore for every man at sea.

The museum was started by a group of people living locally, who formed themselves into the Scottish Fisheries Museum Trust in 1968. The following year the first part of the museum was opened. It quickly won a number of awards and a well-deserved reputation. It is housed in a group of old buildings overlooking the harbour, which itself

Herring girl tableau, detail

has a long association with the industry. The last owners ran a ships' chandlering business, with parts of the building let out as fishermen's stores and net lofts, and nets were barked and dried in the cobbled courtyard.

The visitor enters through the courtyard, which is now filled with an evocative assembly of boats, ropes, barrels, anchors, and the iron wheelhouse and galley saved from 'Brighter Hope III' of 1964 when it was refitted. The main rooms are arranged chronologically, starting with the days of sail and leading to the seine net fishing of the 1920s and later purse seining.

The displays are made up of a number of different elements, which combine to great effect. There is a good collection of ships' models, and pictures range from sophisticated paintings by Victorian artists to primitive works by the seamen themselves. (The

View of the courtyard

urge to create models and pictures of their boats is a characteristic of seafaring men, no doubt by reason of enforced leisure at sea and the relationship between a man and the vessel to which he entrusts his life.) There are old photographs, and occasionally costumed figures acting the parts of the cooper or the herring girl. There are panels bearing accounts of local superstitions or sayings connected with the fishing. There are lamps, harpoon logs, galley stoves, nets and ropes.

In the biggest room we are met with wooden roof timbers and floorboards, spotlit semi-darkness and a slight smell of tar. The room is devoted to the age of steam, and steam drifters and trawlers. In a building on the other side of the courtyard is a reconstruction of a typical fisherman's living room of about the turn of the century. Upstairs is a noble collection of baskets and other tack.

For most of us outside the fisheries the dominating feature is the terrible hardships and dangers faced by the seamen. This is not brought home at Anstruther with quite the same force as it is at **Eyemouth** or **Stromness**, but a present and tragic reminder is the Memorial to Scottish Fisherman Lost at Sea, which is housed in the museum.

There is also an aquarium to see, and in the harbour itself are two boats belonging to the museum. One is the 'Research', a 'Zulu' fishing boat (so-called because they were first built at Lossiemouth at the time of the Zulu war of 1879) which is being restored. The other is the 'Reaper', a 'Fifie' from the turn of the century in full sailing order. And under a lively museum management it is quite likely that by the time this guide is published other acquisitions will be made or in prospect.

AUCHINDRAIN (S)

Auchindrain Open Air Museum of Country Life

Auchindrain, Inveraray, Argyll
PA32 8XN   (04995) 235
Closed October to Easter. ⚡ 🖵 🅿
♿ S
🚻 & ♟ welcome, preferably book in advance.

The name 'Museum of Country Life' is misleading. You'll certainly find here the kind of tools that were used on the land in the Highlands, like ploughs, harrows and seed drills, as well as the ungainly turnip choppers, the distinctive Highland 'flaughter' spade, and the spade with the broad cross member to lean your weight against. But we can see these elsewhere, and the persistent visitor to blackhouses and other croft houses and folk museums may indeed become all too familiar with them. We can also see elsewhere examples of the Highland croft house with a hole in the middle of the roof to let out the smoke from the peat fire, or the genuine 'blackhouse' with no hole at all so that the thatch developed into potash to be dug into the ground for the next season.

What is unique to Auchindrain is the preservation, much as it survived at the end of its effective life, of a whole farming village which in its heyday supported a self-contained community of some six families. (It was probably one of about six such communities in the area between Auchindrain and Inveraray.) At the core of the township were the buildings, and it takes no more than ten minutes or so to walk from the grandest of the dwellings at the top, where the registrar lived, to the humble one-roomed cottage called Bell Pol's house at the other end. Around this core was the best cultivable land, with other arable land outside and, beyond that, grazing land and a quarry for turf, important as a build-

The 'Reaper'

ing material, with the 'airidh' or summer grazing land in the hills behind. The whole township covered an area of some 4,000 acres.

To one side is the oldest of the cottages, built around 1700. The interior shows the life style of the Scottish 'cottar' (landless labourer). The thatch, made of common rush which abounds in the land around, was partly blown away during the winter of 1987/8 and by the following September repair was still waiting for the rushes to grow to a usable size.

The smithy is fully equipped, with the bellows still working and all the astonishing number and variety of tongs and pincers, jacks and metal saws required by the blacksmith. William Stewart recorded his name on one of the beams in 1923, and A. Black did the same in 1935.

Going from one house to another the visitor becomes aware of the varying social status of their occupants. The furnishing of the interiors, as we now see them, is necessarily a matter of museum reconstruction, and we are made all the more critical about its degree of plausibility by the undoubted authenticity of the whole situation. This authenticity, too, raises problems for the curator, and questions about the way the museum visitor sees the past. Auchindrain is not a 'time capsule' for lovers of the picturesque. The old thatch on some of the buildings was replaced by galvanised iron when it became available in the second half of the last century. It was unsightly but practical, one of the signs of continuous change in a poor community. It serves as a reminder that the village was still a working community until the last man, Eddie MacCallum, retired in 1962, and within a year or two plans to preserve it were under way. And the intention has been that so far as possible the old country skills should be kept alive (thatching is a necessity in any case), and that the land in the immediate vicinity of the houses should be worked.

At the entrance to the museum site is a visitor centre, which contains an introductory display covering some of the country crafts that were practised at

General view

The blacksmith's shop

Auchindrain and in similar communities, with dyeing and weaving much in evidence. It also includes photographs of the visit made to Auchindrain by Queen Victoria in 1875. Literature about crofting in the Highlands is on sale, including an excellent illustrated history of Auchindrain and an account

of the life of the inhabitants, with details of the use to which the various buildings were put. The Bank of Scotland has thoughtfully provided a number of golfing umbrellas to shelter visitors as they tour the buildings on the not infrequent occasions when the day is wet.

BIGGAR (S)

Gladstone Court Museum

Biggar ML12 DT (0899) 21050
Closed November to Easter. 🗢
♿: ramp for wheelchairs available.
♟ & ♙ welcome but must book in advance; reduced prices.

Gladstone Court is the brainchild of the Curator, Brian Lambie, who opened it in 1968 in an old coachworks behind his ironmonger's shop (it has since been extended). It is a reconstruction of Victorian Biggar, especially its shops, which are put together in the form of streets and 'pends', as the narrow covered streets in Scottish towns are called. There is the clockmaker; the shoemaker with top boots and leather-working tools; an alley presided over by a hideous portrait of Walter Scott advertising jams and jellies. In the chemist's is the old jar for leeches near to the rows of drawers with their (not always mysterious) gilded labels: 'BISM:TAB:', 'POT:BI-CARB:', 'TOOTH:BRUS:'.

If the milliner and military tailor show only their shop windows, part of the attraction is that we are allowed to go into so many of the shops: into the bank where we can browse through the old ledgers, or into the printer's, or the old telephone exchange, or the little library up a narrow stairway.

The shops and other premises are ingeniously compressed into very confined spaces in such a way that they

Columbia printing press

View of the main 'street'

Chemist's shop, 1860–80

combine the charm of the old world with the fascination of the dolls' house. Some of the reconstructions are composite. The grocer's shop, for example, is based on the shop of William Inglis, but the exterior pillars came from a rival of his, William Ovens, and were first erected in 1879; most of the interior fittings came from two other local shops, and the oldest item, an early 19th century stoneware whisky jar, is from the stock of yet a fourth.

A leaflet provides information about where the separate parts of the display came from, starting with the stone archway of 1650 from old Ingraston House, with asides on the personalities involved in the shops and other buildings. The museum shop also offers a range of booklets on subjects that are relevant to the period of the museum displays, especially when they have a local bearing.

At different points in the booths we are provided with typewritten notes or old photographs, things that contribute to an understanding of the situation as it was. Such is the coherence of the whole display that these are added in without striking a false note.

Comparatively few of the items in the museum are of any monetary value. It is almost as if it had been a point of honour to avoid them because, like Councillor Murray's original **Museum of Childhood** in **Edinburgh**, it was not intended to be that kind of museum. Many things are familiar enough, down to the shop-window model of the woman scrubbing a little boy's ears with Pears soap. We may have seen them in a number of places elsewhere in Britain. Although this might mean that there is little to interest people who come from outside Biggar, it is in fact very revealing to see how these commercial, mass-produced things were absorbed into the culture of a Victorian market town in Scotland without destroying its individual character.

There is besides the distinctive fascination of the museum itself. In effect the whole display is a kind of folk art – a walk-in collage lovingly put together. The result is a rewarding entertainment. But it contains an undeniable element of nostalgia for the older visitor. People who share the belief of Mr Gradgrind in Dickens's *Hard Times* that 'facts alone are wanted in life' will do well to stay away.

Gladstone Court was the first museum established by what is now the Biggar Museum Trust, along with the *John Buchan Heritage Centre* at Broughton. The Trust has since opened two other museums in Biggar itself: the *Greenhill Covenanters' House*, concerned with the 17th century, and the *Moat Park Heritage Centre* for a slightly more conventional and much more comprehensive review of the history of the upper part of Clydesdale and Tweeddale.

BLANTYRE (S)

David Livingstone Centre

Blantyre, Glasgow G72 9BT
(0698) 823140
Open daily. ⑨ ▣ open April to September. ℗
♿ **ST**: access to top floors of main museum is by spiral staircase only.
🛉 & 🛉 contact the Warden; reduced prices.

For anyone inclined to think of David Livingstone vaguely as an African explorer, the David Livingstone Centre is the place to put the record straight.

Livingstone was born here in 1813, and worked in the cotton mill at Blantyre until he went to Glasgow at the age of 23. This was in order to study medicine, as the first stage towards achieving his life's ambition to be of benefit to mankind. The guide book, 'Dr Livingstone: Man of Africa', is helpful and informative. Also available, and perhaps almost more illuminating, is a reprint of Livingstone's own account of his life from 1813 to 1843.

In Livingstone we meet the terrible intellectual crisis that faced a number of young men, not only in Scotland, in the early decades of the last century. These were men brought up with a

Some of Livingstone's notebooks

Young Livingstone working at the mill, from a series of murals by A. E. Haswell Miller

There follows a more conventional museum section. This has the advantage that Livingstone had become a national hero in his own lifetime, with the result that not only his body but a great deal of his equipment and personal belongings were reverently brought home from Zambia, and these things are still preserved for us. They are well displayed, and there is an intelligent use of two levels of information in the labelling, so that you can either go through at a fairly superficial level or linger over the aspects of his life in Africa that interest you most. This may be for example Livingstone the missionary and his medical knowledge and resources, which are explained on a recorded tape, or it may be Livingstone the explorer and the harrowing evidence he saw of the treatment of slaves by their African captors.

The visitor leaves the building by way of a shrine to his memory, where the contributions made by many organisations are recorded. It contains also the best of the carvings by Pilkington Jackson, an evocation of the African bearers carrying Livingstone's coffin through the jungle.

Across a park at a little distance is a modern group of three pavilions: a restaurant, a shop, and the Africa Pavilion, which houses a new exhibition each season on modern Africa.

strong religious faith who were at the same time endowed with a strong bent for science, at the moment when scientific investigation was leading to conclusions that were seen – by Livingstone's father among many others – to be in direct conflict with religious dogma.

Going round the Centre, the visitor comes first to a small museum (the Shuttlerow Museum), which deals with the history of cotton manufacture and the Blantyre mill, started in 1785, and includes the schoolroom where the young David Livingstone was taught. The main focus of the Centre however is the building distinguished on the outside by two semicircular stairwells, which contains 24 single-room tenements (known as 'single ends') including the one where the Livingstones lived.

The building was restored and opened as a memorial in 1929, and the displays have quite recently been renewed. It would be hard not to be moved by this story of the boy whose grandparents had come here from the Hebrides in 1792, and who propped up a Latin primer where he could read it in snatches while he worked at the

spinning jenny from 6 am to 8 pm, first as a 'piecer' at the age of ten and later as a spinner.

The Livingstones' single-end is very well presented, partly because much of the furniture on display was theirs, including the 'wag at the wa' clock', which is kept relentlessly ticking. There is a tape recording describing how people lived in these conditions, cramped and frugal but in no way insalubrious. Further on are a reconstruction of the mill with young Livingstone at his machine, and a crude but effective diorama of his first missionary post at Kuruman in Bechuanaland, where he went in 1841.

On the lower floor of the building the visitor is taken first past eight coloured relief carvings cast in concrete by the late Pilkington Jackson, depicting salient incidents from Livingstone's life in Africa. They are presented as stage sets which the visitor is required to light up one at a time. It is a little difficult to see the value of this somewhat melodramatic form of presentation, except in the scene of Livingstone's death, which exploits the difference between a lantern and the daylight outside the bungalow.

C. d'O. Pilkington Jackson, The Last Journey

BO'NESS (C)

Bo'ness Heritage Trust

Bo'ness Station, Bo'ness, West Lothian EH51 0AD
(0506) 825855
Open at weekends Easter to end October and mid-week during summer (contact Trust office for further details). ▣
&; Birkhill Clay Mine unsuitable for the disabled.
⋔ & ⋔ welcome but must book in advance: contact Trust office, 86a North Street, Bo'ness EH51 9NF

Bo'ness Railway

Bo'ness, pronounced like Bowness in the Lake District, is an abbreviation of Borrowstounness. It looks like a coastal town that flourished in the 19th century, whose industrial role has now declined, but this is deceptive. Bo'ness trade was actually at its peak in the 17th century, although few buildings survive to remind us of this. In the 18th century it was still one of the three busiest Scottish seaports. The harbour and docks, which lie beside the railway station, are now silted up with no immediate prospect of recovery.

The Bo'ness Heritage Trust is organising a big, complex project, the first stage of which will be open for Easter 1989; further developments are likely to be fairly rapid.

The site for future heritage area developments is beside the railway station, which has been reconstructed by the Scottish Railway Preservation Society. In 1988 it contained a display illustrating the history of the Scottish Railway companies before nationalisation. The Society is extremely active, relying as is usual with railway preservation societies on enthusiastic volunteers. It was able to save from Haymarket Station in Edinburgh the Victorian train shed of 1842 that now stands with its elegant low arches and iron supporting columns over the Bo'ness station platform. The station building itself was formerly at Wormit on the south side of the Tay Bridge. The Society also collects, and restores

as far as possible to working order, an extensive range of historic locomotives, carriages and wagons which are housed at the station.

The Bo'ness Heritage Trust is independent of the Railway Preservation Society, but works in close co-operation with it. Trains will be running regularly during the season, taking visitors past Kinneil and the *Kinneil Museum*, and actually cutting through the line of the Roman Antonine Wall before reaching Birkhill Clay Mine. Although the mine can be reached by road, it is a narrow country road, and visitors are encouraged to take the more commodious and entertaining steam train route.

Interior view of the Birkhill clay mine

The clay mine is at present the main feature provided by the Trust itself. A visit to the mine is a great deal more rewarding – and of much less specialised interest – than one might expect. The steam train takes you to Birkhill Station, which has been completed by reconstructing there an attractive wood-and-iron Victorian station building saved from Monifieth, to the east of Dundee.

Just above the station are the buildings, now looking much the worse for the attentions of vandals and scrap merchants, of the clay milling plant that processed the fireclay from the mine. The underground operation at Birkhill was comparatively short-lived, begun in 1911 and closed in 1980 because the demand for Scottish fireclays had fallen off by that date.

The visitor follows a newly-built stairway down a long and precipitous slope to the River Avon, and round into the mouth of the drift entrance to the mine. The stairway runs alongside a cable railway which used to bring up the trucks, or 'hutches', carrying the clay from the mine. This is a rewarding walk in itself, for the way leads down into a highly picturesque gorge in an area of ancient woodland, now protected as a Site of Special Scientific Interest.

The experience of going into a mine is usually associated with low, narrow, damp and dark tunnels, strongly evocative of the miners' working conditions but rarely much more. Birkhill offers an altogether different kind of experience.

The clay that was being mined was fireclay, so rocklike in its natural form that it had to be blasted out with explosives (it is valuable to industry in its treated form for the high temperatures it is able to resist). Although the mine in fact never employed more than 18 men at any one time, and latterly only four, the workings themselves are extremely sizeable with about six miles of passageways. The galleries cut through the clay are high and wide, and the flooring, treacherous while the mine was in operation, has been made safe for visitors with gravel. The method of extraction was the very wasteful one of 'stoop and room', whereby 60% of the usable clay had to be left behind in between the galleries to hold up the roof and the ground above it.

The visitor is taken on a tour, which lasts about 25–30 minutes, through an extensive range of these galleries. They are well lit by electricity. One area is so high that it was known as 'the cathedral'. It is particularly interesting to be able to see formations of fossils in the ground overhead, even the contours of whole fossilised trees.

Besides the clay mine, the most imminent future development at Bo'ness will be a '1920s township'. A pair of Victorian workmen's cottages standing in what is now derelict land beside the old railway station is being restored, and other buildings (the old Co-op shop from nearby Stenhousemuir is already designated) will be brought together on an authentic town plan to recreate the living conditions of the 1920s in a kind of Scottish counterpart to the North of England Open Air Museum at Beamish, Co. Durham.

Further in the future is a plan to convert the large warehouse of the Distillers' Company, near Kinneil Station, partly as a more conventional museum display, and partly as a much needed store for industrial machinery collected by *Falkirk Museum* and by the National Museums.

CERES (F)

Fife Folk Museum

The Weigh House, Ceres, Cupar, Fife KY15 5NF   (033 482) 380
Closed November to Easter, otherwise closed Tuesdays. 🅿
♿ except for interior stair to lower floor.
🅿 & 👥 reduced admission charge if booked in advance.

The approach is unusual. The area behind the museum was cleared to make a large car and coach park, so the visitor usually reaches the museum from the back. The old buildings rising up in front of the clearing have almost the appearance of a film set. The way crosses a stream by the old hump-backed pack horse bridge, 'Bishop's Brig', and continues a few paces up the old High Street. The museum is housed in the weigh house of 1673 and two adjoining 18th century weavers' cottages. The old doorway carries a stone carving of a weigh beam in its pediment, and the words 'GOD

Royal souvenirs

The Weigh House and adjoining cottages

BLESS THE JUST'. The building was originally known as the Jougs, from the French for a yoke, the old Scots name for the iron collar that was worn as a punishment; it served as court house and gaol and also as the place where the rents, paid to the landlord in agricultural produce, were measured.

The weigh house and cottages were restored and converted into a museum of the folk life of Fife, which was opened in 1968. It is the work of a dedicated group of volunteers, and their affection and respect for the old way of life is apparent in the museum they have created. This is the old Kingdom of Fife with its proudly independent spirit, and you are made to feel that however much may be shared with other parts of Scotland and elsewhere, it is the ways of rural Fife that you are being shown. The museum has won four awards, the crown being a Europa Nostra Diploma of Merit in 1985 for 'admirable restoration and adaptation through voluntary dedication' of the buildings. In spite of this, and although Ceres is only two and a half miles from Cupar, one of the busiest centres of Fife, the tourist can easily miss Ceres by being seduced round the coast.

Inside the weigh house we are brought close to reality by a display of the various methods used for weighing and measuring. The familiar type of shop scales, seen alongside the earlier contrivances, bring home the extent to which fair dealings in an ordered society have always relied on accurate systems of measurement. There is con-

View inside cottage showing stair linking the Weigh House

COATBRIDGE (S)

Summerlee Heritage Trust

*West Canal Street, Coatbridge
ML5 1QD   (0236) 31261*
Open daily. ☐ ☐
♿ to all indoor areas, ♿ to some
areas of outdoor exhibits;
wheelchair available for free loan.
♨ & ♟ please book in advance;
education/meeting room available.
☺

Summerlee Heritage Park, with a site
of 25 acres, is one of the undertakings
on an extensive scale, like the **Maritime Museum** at **Irvine**, the **Heritage Area, Bo'ness** and the **Scottish
Mining Museum, Newtongrange**,
that are designed to record between
them Scotland's industrial heritage.
The particular remit at Coatbridge is
stated to be: the social history of the
workers and their families, which is
focused on the Coatbridge district, and
the preservation of 'any machinery so
long as it works and it's Scottish' (but
with close collaboration with the other
industrial museums to avoid duplica-
tion, as in the matter of railway preservation, ships or mining gear).

Coatbridge lies on the eastern edge
of Glasgow, formerly one of the focal
points of British empire trade and
often known as the 'iron burgh'. It has
suffered seriously from the decline of
heavy industry, and this project is part
of an ambitious programme of invest-
ment in tourism and cultural development by Monklands District Council,
contributing to the economic regenera-
tion of the whole area.

Although the project was not started
until late in 1984, many of the elements planned for the Park were
already in place by the summer of
1988. A vast shed of 130,000 sq ft,
which was used up to the early 1950s
by a firm manufacturing cranes, is
taken up partly with the museum workshop and partly with a display of early
19th century machinery, including re-

siderable emphasis on the skilled
trades, such as joiner, reed thatcher,
tinsmith, plasterer, not all of which
have yet vanished. The tools are set out
clearly, rather than in evocative dis-
order or decorative array, and enough
description or illustration is provided
to make sense of the work that is, or
was, involved in these trades. The figure of a wretched prisoner huddled
below is a reminder of the discomforts
of the old gaol. This is characteristic of
the way the original functions of the
buildings have been woven into the
purposes of the museum.

Household things from the early
part of last century have been installed
in one of the cottages – a fireplace with
its kettles and flat iron, and a box bed
occupied by a frail old man with the
goodwife sitting beside him. Authenticity of detail has been assured by
basing the scene on an early 19th
century painting by David Wilkie, who
was brought up a few miles away in
Pitlessie.

Further on are costumes, including a
fine ribbed silk gown from a family in
Ceres, and displays on the crafts of
lace-making and patchwork, and the
fine designs of hand-woven linen. The
familiar assortment of 'bygones' is en-

livened by the presence of a curious
beer-bottling machine and the engaging inventiveness of early vacuum
cleaners. A stair leads down to collections from other trades, and a terrace
beside the stream at the back is used
for a display mainly of farm implements.

More recently an old bothy (one-
roomed cottage) on the other side of
the road, which was damaged by fire,
has been redesigned and rebuilt as an
extension to the museum. It is sensi-
tively restored, like the other museum
buildings, with a nice balance between
retaining original features and adapting
to its new function. The display inside
is devoted mainly to methods of transport, from horses' harness to penny
farthings and a Victorian baby carriage,
and outdoor sports like curling and
croquet.

The museum has a good collection
of old photographs of the district on
show, and there is a nicely produced
and informative guidebook. At the
same time it is well to remember that
the person who sells you your entry
ticket is likely to be a volunteer who has
long resided in Ceres and can tell you a
lot about the way of life represented in
the museum.

constructions of workshops to show what the working life in them was like, and of the old 'steamies' (the public wash-houses).

There is a considerable atmosphere in the long series of workshops with the belt drive running, and the intention is that there will always be some machines working whenever there are visitors. The largest piece of machinery so far installed is the winding engine from Cardowan Colliery, which was built at Coatbridge and has been restored by Summerlee's engineering team.

Just outside this vast shed the visitor looks down onto the recently excavated remains, mostly not very much above ground level, of the old Summerlee ironworks, which were opened in 1835. A section of James Watt's Monklands Canal, which ran alongside to carry the raw materials and finished products, has been restored. Boats such as a replica of Scotland's first iron boat, the 'Vulcan', a passenger boat launched into the canal in 1819, or the steam launch 'Firequeen', will be on display when not on visits to other waters.

Preparations are now far advanced, too, for a working electric tramway to take visitors round the whole site. A

The tram for visitors

group of workers' houses removed from elsewhere on the site now stand at the entrance. [These contain a shop, meeting room and exhibition space; an historic office building reclaimed from nearby Whifflet now houses the tearoom. Ed.] Over on the other side,

the entrance to a small drift mine (one that is approached at ground level), of a kind that was once common all over central Scotland, is being reconstructed, and will lead to an underground exhibition including a beam engine originally built in 1810.

There is admittedly no way of recreating the 'experience' of a blast furnace. Short of that, however, the intention is that the visitor should be brought as near as possible to understanding what these former 'workshops of the British Empire' were like, and what it was like to be living beside them and working in them.

Besides its commitment to collecting evidence on Scotland's industrial past, the Trust sets out to serve another purpose: to provide interest and entertainment for visitors of all ages, not just the industrial archaeologist and the machinery buff. On its present showing, it seems likely to achieve it.

[Boats are now restored in a boatshop on the banks of the Monklands Canal, and workshop sessions allow volunteers to learn the arts of wooden boatbuilding. Other workshops include rag-rug making, and there are special events and regular steaming of crane and steam rollers. Ed.]

The workshops

CREETOWN (D)

Creetown Gem-Rock Museum

Chain Road, Creetown,
Kirkcudbrightshire
(0671 82) 357
Open daily. 🔊🖼️🅿️♿
👫 & 🚻 welcome but must book in advance.

The unattractive building belies the magical sights that lie inside. This was an old school house that had been made into a general museum, which included a section of gem rocks. In 1980 it was taken over by the Stephenson family from Yorkshire, who use it partly as a museum, now devoted entirely to their collection of gemstones, minerals and other rock samples, and partly as their workshop and shop for the production and sale of things they make from gemstones. At the entrance there is a window onto the workshop, where the craftsmen carry on their business of cutting and working the stones.

Rock crystal

Geode from Brazil

The collection is a profusion of gemstones from all over the world, arranged mainly according to their type or place of origin. Not much effort is put into elegant labelling or the latest museum techniques. The whole preoccupation of the family, and the whole interest of the visitor, is taken up with the appearances of the stones themselves, whether in their raw state, or cut and polished, or turned to some usable or decorative purpose. Explanations are at a minimum (but remember, the man you speak to is likely to be one of the family, and not only extremely knowledgeable but keen to share his knowledge with you).

The gemstones are the thing. And brilliant things they are, absorbing to look at even for those who know nothing about them. There are plenty of strikingly beautiful natural shapes and colours, and there is the craftsmanship to be admired, mostly in handsome and unpretentious work.

There is a case of stones collected by the Stephensons in 1983 on a visit to Majorca and Almeria in Southern Spain, to an old mining area that contained copper, silver and iron, where Hannibal once financed expeditions for gold and silver. There is a tall, dazzling white rock crystal; a piece of gypsum 'desert rose' of Texas chalcedony, with extraordinary slivers projecting at all angles like the leaves of a cactus; 'fool's gold' from Peru, with its silver facets made of iron pyrite; and a huge geode from Brazil, a shapeless, dull-looking lump of rock split open to reveal a glittering amethyst cavern inside.

A large and spectacular display shows the fluorescent properties of certain stones. Seen under normal light, they are dull and monochromatic in appearance. Under ultra-violet light they become iridescent with intense blues and violets, scarlet, dark red and brilliant green.

There are separate displays of jade, rose quartz, amethyst, marble, agate, petrified wood, malachite, silver and lead galena. There are stones from India, Africa, Peru, Norway, America, Brazil, Turkey. There are lumps of alabaster from Nottinghamshire, jet from Whitby, coral from Scotland.

Scotland is given her due place in this international gathering. When the famous Scots geologist Hugh Miller was a boy in Cromarty, he picked up from the beach a fragment of garnet crystals embedded in mica-schist. It was, he thought, just like a brooch of his mother's, but the neighbours explained patronisingly that his mother's brooch was made of precious stones, whereas his find was nothing but 'a stone upon the shore'. Fortunately his Uncle Sandy knew better, and we too learn better at Creetown. Near the case of stone from Almeria is another containing stones found on the beach or in the burn at Creetown – agate in basalt, malachite, galena, quartz, amethyst, coloured granite. It is a startling range, shown raw and worked, many examples having one face polished flat to show the coloured grain. Gemstones found elsewhere in Scotland include amethyst, agate, beryl, cairngorm, chalcedony and hornblende.

Gypsum 'desert rose' of Texas chalcedony

DOUNE (C)

Doune Motor Museum

Doune, Perthshire FK16 6HD
(0786) 841 203
Closed November to March. 🔊 📺
🅿 ♿

Some of the museum's cars, a Bugatti Type 57C, 1938, and Jaguar SS 100, 1937, in the foreground

This museum is less than twenty years old and grew, like so many of the best museums, out of the personal enthusiasm of one man – the Earl of Moray, descendant of the Bonnie Earl who was brutally murdered in 1591. The family seat was the splendid Doune Castle nearby, which is now open to visitors under the Scottish Development Department.

In 1953 Lord Moray answered an advertisement for a 1934 Type 26 Hispano-Suiza. This was to be the first item in the museum, but he bought the car to drive it, and any idea of forming a museum was still several years away. In fact his next purchase was not until 1961/2, when he bought an Invicta, an Abbot Bentley, an SS 100 Jaguar and an 8 CM Maserati for use in hill climbing competitions.

In 1968 the Doune Hill Climb Course was opened. By then, Lord Moray had made several further purchases, and the need to house them in satisfactory conditions and the interest shown by motoring buffs persuaded him to convert a group of farm buildings near the Hill Climb Course into a museum. This was opened in 1970.

It is a motor museum, but you will not find here explanations of how the internal combustion engine works, or the history of its invention and subsequent refinements. Nor will you find the sorts of cars that were regularly seen on our roads 30 or 50 years ago – the Austin 7s, the Morris Minors, the Ford Populars. The cars here – about 40 in total – were either born great or have achieved greatness, with the exception of the ill-fated Sinclair C5, which no doubt qualified for inclusion by having greatness thrust upon it.

The cars are shown off at their best, all in immaculate condition, as if they had never been driven over a dusty roadway. Beside each is a brief but clear account of its history, often not merely the history of the type but the story of that particular vehicle. There is no mistaking the thoroughness and accuracy of the research involved, but care has been taken not to overwhelm the visitor with information.

The senior citizen here is the second oldest Rolls-Royce in the world, made in 1905 (ill. on cover). In 1920, when it belonged to a man in Kilmarnock, it alarmed a horse, which shied at it and kicked in the offside. Another of the

Hispano-Suiza 37.2 h.p., 1924

Sunbeam 3 litres, 1913 (on loan from Kenneth Lawrie)

earlier cars is the Sunbeam racing car, with its handsome wheels with spokes and rims of varnished wood. It was bought new in 1913 for the son of a Galloway family, who was killed in the Great War. His mother ordered it to be buried, and it was only disinterred when it was struck by a plough, like the Mildenhall treasure; it has now been splendidly rebuilt.

Side by side with these superb examples of design and craftsmanship, a place is kept for more modest examples of sheer inventiveness, in which elegance and panache played no part. One of these is a small racing car designed for lightness, and weighing about half as much as a Mini, which is one of about twelve designed and built by Joseph Potts in Scotland in 1958. It should perhaps be said that there is quite a high proportion of racing cars in the collection, a result of the very way in which new designs are brought out and tested as much as of the particular enthusiasm of Lord Moray.

Most of the exhibits date from between the 1930s and the early 1970s. For the afficionado they need no justification. For the layman they are objects of distinction and beauty regardless of what they have under the bonnet. They take their places in the history of taste and fashion, contribut-ing to the wider field of social history by their power to evoke, like the Eton crop and the Charleston, the society for which they were created.

For a small independent museum in the country, the design of the whole establishment is to a very high standard, most of it a conversion of old farm buildings, which are still recognisable from the outside. The interior is completely modernised – clean and spacious with a red composition floor and a system of track lighting overhead, to match the immaculate condition of the exhibits. These are a little like horses in a stable, since they are occasionally out at exercise, either competing at vintage race meetings or taking part in the hill climbs and other events that are held here in April, June and September. Besides this, there are always a number of cars here on loan, like the Sunbeam and the early Rolls, which belongs to the Royal Scottish Automobile Club.

As you emerge from the exhibition itself, you come into a flourishing shop, and while comparatively few of the articles on offer have any connection with the museum, except for a well illustrated guide, their sale is clearly an important factor in its survival. Opposite to it is a spacious cafeteria which serves hot meals.

DUMFRIES (D)

Dumfries Museum & Camera Obscura

The Observatory, Dumfries
DG2 7SW   (0387) 53374
Closed Sundays and Mondays
October to March. ▣
♿: access to all parts except windmill.

The original museum building was an 18th century windmill tower. Threatened with demolition in 1834, it was saved by a public appeal and put into service as an observatory and camera obscura two years later. The camera obscura still operates to give panoramas of the surroundings. An unusual feature is the spiral staircase at one side of the circular building, whose wooden centre pole leans inwards following the slope of the outer wall.

The intention to incorporate a museum seems to have grown up almost immediately, and at first informally. It is therefore one of the oldest public collections in Scotland, and it once boasted among its exhibits, in keeping with early museological ambitions, a fragment claimed to come from the Tower of Babel. Now painted white, the building is a conspicuous and attractive feature of the Dumfries landscape. In 1862 an extension was built, which added a main exhibition

Fragment of gold brooch with filigree work

The observatory building

hall. This was to house the collections of the Dumfriesshire and Galloway Natural History and Antiquarian Society, which had been recently founded.

The museum today retains much of the fascination of the old kind of miscellaneous collection, although it has been arranged in such a way as to avoid the bewildering confusion that could sometimes prevail. The remit of the museum is the whole of the history and natural history of the Dumfries and Galloway region. It is not for those in a hurry, or for those who prefer to be fed by a spoon.

Among the more rare archaeological finds from the district is the fragment of a gold brooch with extremely delicate filigree work. There is also a model of a 'crannog', the type of Iron Age dwelling that was built in large numbers offshore in the lochs of Scotland. The natural history section has a good display of the birds found round the Solway. A section on geology contains examples of the rather beautiful iron nodule sandstone, which is rare outside the Dumfries basin.

A delightful reminder of the enviable confidence of earlier archaeologists is a bronze pot found in Lochend Loch near the coast in 1852, which is now known to date from the Middle Ages. The pot itself is engraved, within an elegantly scrolled border, with the name of the donor and a description beginning: 'This Ancient Roman Brass Pot . . .'.

Characteristic of Galloway and the south west of Scotland are the stones with natural holes in them, which were hung up as a protection against witches (Dumfries retained a belief in withcraft longer than most other parts of Scotland). But perhaps for many visitors the most interesting things are to be found in the 19th century collection related to Dumfries and its neighbourhood. Here is a magnificent ten gallon punchbowl given to the seven trades to commemorate the opening of the Trades Hall in 1806 (ill. on cover); and, by contrast, the death mask of Robert Smith, the last man to be executed in public in Scotland, hanged in Dumfries in 1868 for the murder of an 11-year-old girl.

The world's first pedal bicycle, built about 1840 by Kirkpatrick MacMillan, a blacksmith working a few miles outside Dumfries, no longer exists, but the museum has a copy made by an apprentice wheelwright as he remembered the bicycle from seeing it as a small boy. There is a collection of Victorian dresses and a series of topographical pictures of the neighbourhood. A good collection of farm implements, including mantraps and spring guns, saddlery, blacksmithing and carpentry tools, is in the lower part of the mill building. Higher up is an extremely elegant Gregorian telescope made in Kilmarnock for the Observatory when it was opened in 1836.

A further extension was added in 1981, and the three parts of the building each have their own distinctive characteristics. By then the museum had been taken over by the local authority, now Nithsdale District Council, and it has absorbed a number of smaller independent museums that have had to close, including the Grierson Museum at Thornhill and the Langholm Museum.

Medieval bronze pot found in Lochend Loch

DUNBEATH (H)

Laidhay Croft Museum

Dunbeath, Caithness KW6 6EH
(05933) 244
Closed October to Easter. 🔊 🅿
♿; stable and byre have cobbled
floors but can mostly be seen from
doorway.
🚹 & 🚻 welcome but must book in
advance.

The croft house at the Laidhay Croft
Museum is a long, low building with
doors and windows on the south-
eastern side only. It stands on flat, high
ground near the coast. The croft itself
was being worked until 1968. It was
acquired by the Laidhay Preservation
Trust – a photograph taken of the
kitchen at the time when it was taken
over shows the state of the interior –
and was opened as a museum in 1974.

A good leaflet produced by the
Trust, 'The Caithness Croft', includes
a discussion of Laidhay itself and its
relationship to other crofts in the area.
However, the visitor is likely to learn at
least as much or more from the welcoming caretaker, who willingly shares
her knowledge of Caithness crofting
life.

The roof of the barn

Alexander Mackay beside his whisky still

Caithness chairs made from driftwood

One of the distinctive features of the
croft is the barn, which is at a short
distance from the house. As was cus-
tomary, a second door opposite to the
main one was opened to allow a
draught across the barn for winnowing.
There is a flagged floor, Caithness
stone being well adapted by its nature
for making flagstones. The roof is supported by three 'crucks', essentially
arches made of curving timbers. As
wood was scarce, the roof timbers were
made up mainly from driftwood, the
crucks being composed of several
pieces lapped and pegged together. In
both the barn and the house the thatch,
which is laid over a layer of turf on the
roof timbers, is held down at the sides
with boards, whereas in the west of
Scotland it is tied down with ropes
attached to stones.

Inside and outside the barn are farm
implements that were once used in the
area, most of them – like the tools and
other things in the house itself – presented by farmers in the neighbour-

hood. They include rollers, a harrow, ploughs, a grindstone, a turnip slicer and a curious Victorian wooden cart jack.

The living quarters in the house consist of a kitchen and main room, which is divided by a box bed with its open side facing the fire. The room and kitchen are flagged. One of the supports for the roof of the kitchen is a cruck of the lapped and pegged type found in the barn; otherwise the roof timbers are standard cuts that were brought here when the croft house was being restored. The furnishings, like the farm implements, have been given mainly by people from the neighbourhood as characteristic of what would once have been in the house. They suggest a very simple lifestyle, but one of reasonable comfort. There are a number of the distinctive Caithness chairs. These were put together from driftwood, the seats commonly being made up to the required depth with dowels because of the rarity of boards wide enough for the purpose. Books were regarded as permanent sources of wisdom; the two principal books here are a church bible printed in very large type and a copy of Wylie and Anderson's *Scots Worthies*, which belonged to a Mr Nisbet in the middle of last century, printed in the same way.

In cases running behind the box bed is a social history collection. Notable is an interesting photograph taken in about 1920 by an American, Miss Havemeyer, of a certain Alexander Mackay, known as 'Ali Ruardih Mal', who lived at Kintail. He distilled whisky illegally up to 1943 and, by dint of keeping moving, was never caught by the revenue men. He is seen standing beside his still.

At one end of the house is a stable for at least two horses, now used for a display of harness and tack. Like the byre, which is divided from the living quarters by a wooden partition at the other end of the building, the stable is cobbled. A square-section drain made of Caithness slabs runs down the centre of the byre. Above it at the far end is a square opening that used to be blocked by manure that was collected from the byre when in time it fell out onto the midden outside.

DUNDEE (T)

McManus Galleries

Albert Square, Dundee DD1 1DA
(0382) 23141 ext. 65136
Closed Sundays. ☐ ☐ W
☗ & ☗ welcome, preferably book in advance, as above ext. 65134

This building and the displays in it have been undergoing a thorough transformation, like so much of Dundee, in the past decade. It was built in 1867 by George Gilbert Scott to house the library and museum collections of the old Watt Institution, which was founded in 1824. It was then named the Albert Institute as a memorial to the Prince Consort.

The library was moved out recently, releasing the whole building for the museum and art gallery. At the same time it was renamed after Dr Maurice McManus, a former Lord Provost of

Dundee and Labour councillor of long standing who had just died. An information and sales desk and a floor plan of the building are conveniently sited in the entrance hall. The hall then leads into three major galleries, which have been completely redesigned since 1985. Their titles are: 'A Prosperous Burgh', on Dundee's jute, jam and journalism; 'Here's tae Dundee' on the social history of Dundee; and 'Discover your past' on the archaeology of Tayside.

The title 'Discover your past' is a reminder that one of the principal concerns of the museum, perhaps the main one, is to serve the people of Dundee. Visitors from outside Dundee may well find the trade and industry room the most absorbing, since everything there is unique to Dundee: the Tay Bridge and the history of its disaster (including some pathetic mementoes); Valentine's the printers; the D.C. Thomson empire of newspapers from the *Sunday Post* to the *Beano*; the processing first of flax and later of jute from Bengal; marmalade; boat building, particularly

View of main hall on first floor, housing fine and applied art

World's oldest surviving astrolabe, 1555

the whaling ships, since Dundee was to have the biggest whaling fleet in Britain. (There is an excellent display on whaling in the *Broughty Castle Museum*, just outside Dundee.)

The trade union banners are here, too, and this leads us to Dundee's social history. A fine reconstruction of a public-house bar is next door to a 'drunk's barrow', a handcart no doubt appropriately, if ominously, in the shape of a coffin. Other set pieces are a grocery, a tenement kitchen and a middle-class bedroom. One or two historic personalities are celebrated, notably the poetaster William McGonagall. Those with a taste for the macabre will relish a lurid assembly of scolds' bridles from an earlier age. Particularly distinctive is a narrow decorative frieze some 45 feet long, painted for the Company of Cordiners (i.e. shoemakers). It represents a ritual procession of obscure origin and significance, of King Crispin (originally St Crispin the patron saint of the shoemakers) with the figures of a Champion in armour, the Black Prince and others.

The most recently re-opened room is the one devoted to archaeology. Here, too, although special to Tayside, visitors from elsewhere are likely to find much to catch their interest, like the reconstruction of a dwelling from

Douglasmuir in the Lunan Valley, or the Pictish boat, 26 feet long, carved about AD 500 out of a single trunk of oak, or the fine Pictish carved stones. The display sensibly follows the current trend of taking the public behind the scenes, by giving an idea of how the archaeologist works. For example, we gain a clear impression of the successive layers of excavation as we come up to the Roman fortress at Carpow, near Abernethy, and end with photographs as reminders of Norman and Medieval buildings that still survive above ground.

The main hall on the first floor (the grand outside staircase used to lead into it) is now freed of the library stacks and has been restored to its original Victorian gothic splendour. It houses examples of fine and applied arts, ranging from Dundee silver and a beautiful gold snuff mull made in Scotland in about 1725, recently acquired, to a varied collection of glass and works of art brought from the East.

The collection of paintings is also upstairs, now shown in light, spacious galleries. Its strength is in 19th century Scottish art, and it has recently been enriched by an important group of landscapes and subject pictures, including ones by McTaggart, Orchardson and Chalmers (colour plate 2), acquired in 1987 from the Orchar Gallery, a private foundation at nearby Broughty Ferry that had to close for lack of funds. A collection of Scottish contemporary art and photography is being built up. Four of the rooms are reserved for temporary exhibitons. In a pattern that is now becoming fairly common, some of these are on specific themes drawn from the permanent collection, since only a small part of it can be displayed at one time. [One of the galleries that were added to the Albert Institute in 1889 specifically to display paintings has recently been restored: the Victoria Gallery, with terracotta-red walls, contains over 100 paintings hung densely in tiers, with sculptures, cabinets of ceramics and potted palms to add to the 'Victorian' atmosphere. Paintings include works by Rossetti, Millais, and more particularly Scottish 19th century artists. Ed.]

Royal Research Ship 'Discovery'

Victoria Harbour, Dundee DD1 4BU (0382) 201175
Closed October to March. 🛈 🅿
&: inaccessible to wheelchairs, very difficult for the infirm.
🛉 & 🛉 advanced booking is advised, and includes a concessionay price for educational groups.

On 21 March 1986, in a blaze of publicity, the 'Discovery' came back to Dundee from London Dock, carried on another vessel. Where it is now berthed in Victoria Harbour, its masts are visible from many parts of the city and have acted like a banner symbolising the new spirit in Dundee.

The idea of bringing back 'Discovery' was inspired. It was first put forward in a development study prepared for the Scottish Development Agency as one part of a plan to revitalise a city that had been badly hit by unemployment. The Royal Research Ship 'Dis-

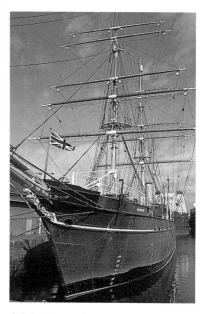

R.R.S. 'Discovery'

covery' was built in Dundee for Captain Scott, and Scott's expedition to the Antarctic set out in it from London early in 1901. The story is well told in the museum's booklet, 'Discovery in Dundee', on the building of the ship and on the expedition.

'Discovery' was Britain's first purpose-built research vessel. Scott went to Dundee to have it built because it had to survive an arctic winter. It was the shipyards where the whalers were built that knew most about withstanding the enormous pressures of drifting pack ice on a ship's hull, and the Dundee whalers were renowned for their strong hulls. The strength of 'Discovery''s hull relied upon a wooden structure, as being more flexible than iron, with two layers of timbers lying across each other at different angles to make up together a thickness of 11 feet. The visitor is shown this quite clearly during the tour of the ship. Visits are in guided parties, and the tour takes about 45 minutes. It is a good indication of the enthusiasm raised by the ship's return to Dundee that a great deal of the guiding is done by volunteers, whose pride in the ship has much in common with the pride of a ship's crew.

The visitor has the fascination of seeing all over the ship itself. (It was in fact modified for later expeditions, but the account of its shortcomings and the improvements that were made to overcome them is itself a part of the story.) Besides this, the dramatic reality of the voyage is powerfully evoked merely by standing in the messroom for the officers and scientists who were on the expedition, with their names on the doors of the cabins that lead off from it. Methods of making the voyage as vivid as possible are always under review; for instance during the summer of 1988 visitors were met on board by actors playing the parts of Captain Scott and members of his crew, who explained some of the difficulties and hardships they had faced.

To a great extent the story of the shipbuilding skills and the hardships that were faced on long winter voyages in the Antarctic is shared by the whalers. We can pick up this trail nearby in

Volunteer guide showing visitors aboard 'Discovery'

the museum at *Broughty Castle* and in other museums along the coast from Whitby in Yorkshire to **Peterhead, Stromness** and **Lerwick**, the ports from which the whaling crews went out. Perhaps least like a museum of them all is 'Discovery' itself. It was brought to Dundee by an independent body called the Dundee Heritage Trust, as the first of a series of enterprises they plan for enhancing the

Performance aboard of play, 'Dundee Made'

quality and attractiveness of the city, much of which depends inevitably on raising the necessary funds. Besides the lengthy and costly process of restoring the ship, which is by no means complete, future plans include moving it to another berth some 300 yards away. Re-ordering the route taken round the ship itself is scheduled for 1991, and is planned to include an evocation of the smell and clutter on shipboard. At the same time the onshore part of the display for visitors will be extended and improved.

After the waterfront project and 'Discovery''s move there, future schemes aim to generate 'an exciting voyage of discovery through Dundee's past, present and future'. Next in line is a project to take over one of Dundee's old textile mills to develop a centre for the illustration of the impact of textiles, particularly flax and jute, on the city's economy. After that will come ideas for exploring the area's agriculture, the famous jams and marmalades, engineering and high technology in the place where the first personal computers were produced, and Dundee's contribution to the field of journalism.

EASDALE ISLAND (S)

Easdale Island Folk Museum

Easdale Island, by Oban, Argyll
(08523) 370 (evenings only)
Closed November to March. ⬛
♿ X museum, but access to
Easdale Island from mainland by
passenger ferry boat and difficult
to get on/off when tide low.

Easdale Island is a small island to the
west of Seil Island, south of Oban,
which is reached by ferry boat. The
museum's function in relation to the
island is rather different from that of
other local museums, since without
visiting it the enquiring tourist can
discover very little about Easdale Island and its unusual history.

The island is made of slate, and its
quarries were one of the prime sources
of slate in the 18th and 19th centuries.
Journal no.1 of the Transactions of the
Marble and Slate Co of Netherlorn
was dated 1746. In 1771 Thomas Pen-
nant recorded that by then two and a
half million slates were exported every
year, as far afield as Canada and the
West Indies. By 1842–62 the figure
had risen to seven million.

Then in 1881 disaster struck the
island, when a great storm filled up the
slate quarries and rendered them all
useless except for one that was not very
productive. The recovery of slate continued, but at a much reduced rate,
until the industry on the island ceased
in 1911. Many of the quarrymen left to
seek work elsewhere.

The island has always been privately
owned, and it still is. But whereas it
was owned continuously by the
Breadalbane family until fairly recently, it has changed hands three times
since the 1960s. By 1867 it was nearly
derelict and deserted, most of the cottages being roofless. The new owner
then began the work of restoration and
of encouraging people to return. His
successor in 1979 began to encourage

View of Easdale Island today

Slate quarry, Easdale Island

the collection of old records about the
island and the slate industry there. It
was through his initiative that the
museum was started in 1980, housed
in a modern building that had been
used as a billiard room. In 1988 it was
made into a private trust.

The museum space is crowded with
exhibits, but a division of the room by
screens allows the several aspects of
life that it deals with to be allotted
distinct areas. There is comparatively
little that is particularly rare or valuable. In view of the desertion of the
island at the turn of the century, it is
surprising so much material has been

recovered, most of it coming from the
attics of the quarrymen's cottages –
and still coming to light.

Much of the displays are focussed
on old photographs and documents, or
photographs of documents, and reports
from the *Oban Times* up to 1914. A
good deal relates to the social life of
the 19th century, which is in no way
unique to the island but nevertheless
contributes to the image we get of the
life there. Meanwhile papers, letters,
old bills, lists – the raw material of
history – are sensibly presented in a
way that allows you to pick them up
and read them. These are often more

interesting, and give a livelier picture of the island life than the actual objects on show.

There is for instance the touching account of communicating by telephone with Oban 16 miles away in March 1878, 'speaking and singing being distinctly heard and any change of voice being quite recognisable.' And an inspector visiting the school recorded how in his own day the children had had to bring peats for the schoolroom fire, those who brought none having to sit furthest from the fire. There are records of the friendly societies, the early form of mutual insurance, including for example the rule book of the Easdale Young Men's Friendly Society of 1875; of the strongly teetotal Independent Order of Rechabites; and of the Easdale Volunteer Artillery 1860–1908. Easdale also boasted, like so many other places in Scotland at the time, a Literary and Scientific Association, which was formed in 1869. There are photographs of the quarries, and of islanders posing self-consciously at their cottage doors or in front of houses or on outings in the hills around. And there is a very informative booklet telling the history of the island.

The museum, the collections and the research being done on the island centre on the person of the curator, Mrs Adams, and rely on her enthusiasm for the island. She makes herself available to answer questions, and even more to hear of any prospect of information that is new to her about life on the island. Although she was brought up in the south, her grandfather had worked at Easdale as a quarryman until the disaster of 1881, when he was still only 18; he was one of the many who went to London to find other work.

In cases of this kind, it is tempting to speculate what will become of the museum when the curator and prime mover is no longer there. The Easdale museum will certainly not be the same after Mrs Adams retires from it, and those of us who are privileged to come while she is there to infect us with her enthusiasm must count ourselves lucky.

EDINBURGH (L)

Huntly House Museum

142 Canongate, Edinburgh
EH8 8DD   (031) 225 2424
ext. 6689
Closed Sundays, except during Edinburgh Festival. ▣
&♿ S: difficult for wheelchairs; handrails assist the infirm.
🚻 & ♿ welcome but must book in advance.

At Huntly House the displays in the showcases are perfectionist. Every object, carefully restored or repaired, is treated as a work of art – which indeed it very often is. Police truncheons and muskets of the city guard are arranged in decorative patterns. Weights and measures, once humble everyday vessels for filling with ale, corn or potatoes, are set out tastefully against suitable backgrounds of coloured felt. The message is that these things are works of fine craftsmanship, like the beautiful examples of Edinburgh glass and Edinburgh silver, which we are not surprised to find displayed with this

degree of fastidiousness. The Scots' delight in making and using superb, generously shaped silver spoons – we meet it again in the museum at **Inverness** and elsewhere – is a constant surprise in a nation that has not always been notable for its visual sensitivity.

The museum aims to celebrate the noblest and most distinguished elements of Edinburgh life, the things of which the people of Edinburgh can be proud. Burke and Hare and Deacon Brodie are not here. Even the notorious filth of the streets in the days of *gardez loo* is represented only by the carefully cleaned and polished badge of the 'street overseer', who did his best to sweeten it. Visitors with a taste for the most lurid aspects of Edinburgh life, who are not too fussy about historical accuracy, are better advised to go a little further up the Royal Mile to the Wax Museum. [Wax Museum now closed. Ed.] Meanwhile, a different aspect of Edinburgh, from the 18th century to the present, is to be shown just opposite Huntly House in another of the City's museums, due to open in July 1989, *The People's Story.*

There is a very attractive collection at Huntly House of those crude carved and painted wooden figures that once

Barber's sign of bear, pole and bleeding dish

Coffee pot by William Dempster, 1749

served as shop signs (one ill. on cover). Distinguished among them are a number of kilted highlanders. These figures were a feature of 18th century tobacconists' shops, evidently more common in the south than in Scotland. They advertised snuff, because snuff was a product of the thriving Glasgow trade in tobacco, which was mulled in Scotland. Displays on the history of the city since Roman times include a beautiful model of the High Street as it was at the time of Mary Queen of Scots, and plans of Edinburgh's new town in the late 18th century by James Craig.

As we walk through the panelled rooms, the old floors creaking under our feet, the demands of public safety and museum circulation still leave some sense of what the old rooms were like, and various features of the original building are clearly described as we come to them. An important element of the museum is the fact that it is one of the few old houses of the Canongate, in the old part of Edinburgh, whose interior we are allowed to visit, and anything that illuminates the life lived in the old wynds and closes of the Royal Mile between the Castle and Holyrood is to be welcomed.

The name Huntly House is perhaps

misleading, implying as it does that this was built as a single mansion. Three existing houses were joined together in 1570 and a section above Bakehouse Close was incorporated; the two white-harled upper storeys were built on a hundred years later. The whole complex was restored and opened as a museum in 1932. The present entrance however is via a pair of tenements at the side, dating from 1648, which was incorporated in 1969.

Ingeniously slotted in among the rooms are a few reconstructed scenes: a late 18th century drawing room in Edinburgh's new town (although the restored Georgian House in Charlotte Square now makes this period more of a reality); a working class kitchen of about 1870; a Leith factory for the manufacture of clay pipes of about 1920; and a curious display on the cordiners (shoemakers) with three gilded and trepanned skulls. [The cordiner display can now be seen in *The People's Story*. Ed.]

In 1964 Edinburgh acquired the collection and papers of Field-Marshall Earl Haig from his son, the present Lord Haig. The collection is preserved at Huntly House, and there is a reconstruction of Haig's headquarters at the end of the 1914–18 war.

An attractively written and illustrated booklet describes the house itself and the collection of Edinburgh silver, glass and pottery. It also places Edinburgh in the context of Scottish history.

Artefacts from Roman fort at Cramond

Museum of Childhood

42 High Street, Edinburgh EH1 1TG
(031) 225 2424 ext. 6645
Closed Sundays, except during Edinburgh Festival. ▪
♿: access by lift to 3 out of 5 galleries and T.
▥ & ♛ welcome but must book in advance.
Baby changing facility.

This museum had a delightful beginning, which is very properly celebrated in one of the first showcases you come to. Patrick Murray, an Edinburgh chemist and City Councillor, started a collection illustrating the history of childhood in 1955 when he was in his late forties, although a confirmed bachelor with 'a rooted conviction that children are only tolerable after their baths and on their way to bed'. He also objected to spending any money on the collection, or even on cases to house it, which he begged from other museums. Within two years the collection had grown enough for the Council to give him the present site. Did he intend it to be *for* children or *about* children? The question was perhaps as confused in Councillor Murray's mind as was the mixture of his own childhood memories with his fascination for historical change.

The result was an irresistible profusion of toys, games, dolls, puzzles, books, clothes, which came pouring in as gifts from all sides. Parents, nothing loath to accompany their children, would find their interests diverging, the children being drawn by their natural bloodthirstiness to the peepshows of Sweeney Todd or Madame Guillotine, which are still here in working order.

Councillor Murray died in 1981, and in 1986 the museum, now run by the City Museums Service, was considerably extended and the collections were completely rearranged in new cases, with new descriptive labels. The reconstructed building is complex, but signposting is excellent. A fine Georgian ceiling has been carefully restored, but unfortunately it lacks the

Russian painted wooden skittles

many of which come from one collection, the Lovett Collection. Elsewhere is a beautiful set of Russian painted wood skittles. Among the dolls' houses, pride of place must go to a heroic butcher's shop with its butcher and his assistant (colour plate 4). Among the model railways are some of the early steam and clockwork engines, including a recently acquired steam-powered locomotive made in Germany in 1903/4. Distinctive among the tin soldiers is a beautiful set of tiny domestic figures made from tin in Nürnberg around 1840 in a tradition that goes back to about the 1730s.

It is a museum that has a wealth of things to look at, whatever your age, and it is easy enough to pick out the things that take your eye. The publications available at the bookstall are mostly designed for children, but also include a souvenir guide.

answering space below it since the floor has been raised to make more room. In a complete reversal of Councillor Murray's old principle, no expense was spared in continuing his good work. Much is no doubt gained, and one suspects that many more visitors benefit from the displays, which are very rich in interest. But it is perhaps inevitable that something of the spirit of the original has been allowed to escape.

Every case has a printed panel with brief, clear and helpful descriptive or historical notes on the objects in it (there are sometimes over 80 items in a case). The principle is to let you see them all, rather than to make an exclusive selection on the basis of historic importance or aesthetic value. At times the grouping can have a curiously jarring effect, which is perhaps salutary. A fascinating clockwork cymbal player from France, for example, and clockwork dancers and a strolling couple worked on a flywheel from Germany, all of the late 19th century, stand cheek by jowl with hideous clockwork dancers made in Japan for the European market in the 1930s and a celluloid Cinderella and her Prince Charming of the 1950s.

The original uncertainty as to whether this was a museum for or

about children has somehow never been resolved. To a major extent it is about children's amusements. A small section, largely of engravings and photographs, on children in the mines or sweeping chimneys, and some costumes on the top floor, seem almost out of place among the model railways, toy theatres and Meccano sets. And the section devoted to children's books, which had been a particular interest of Councillor Murray's museum, is now considerably condensed.

A working nickelodeon, that halfway stage between the pianola and the juke box of American origin, is a fascinating museum object, and it makes a splendid noise, even if its relevance to childhood is not entirely clear. There is a very good collection of optical toys, although it is a pity that they are not displayed in such a way that their effect can be seen. However the notes are thorough, and we learn for instance that the kaleidoscope was invented by Sir David Brewster of St Andrews in 1817, who was later closely involved in the early history of photography.

One room is devoted mainly to dolls, and for most of us the profusion is likely to seem counter-productive. Yet there are excellent things, particularly among the dolls from other countries – Russia, Africa, Egypt, India, Japan –

Papier maché bulldogs, French, c.1910

Swiss musical box, 1915

National Gallery of Scotland

The Mound, Edinburgh EH2 2EL
(031) 556 8921
Open daily. ▣
♿ W except Room A1.
🚼 & 🚻 contact Education Dept. ◉

The permanent collection of the National Gallery was started by the Royal Institution, a group of Scottish noblemen and gentlemen, with the purchase of 30 Italian and Flemish pictures bought in Genoa in 1830, including Van Dyck's big 'Lomellini Family' and 'St Sebastian'. Outstanding among the earliest gifts were the great Tiepolo 'Finding of Moses', Gainsborough's 'Hon Mrs Graham', Allan Ramsay's portrait of his second wife, and Watteau's 'Fêtes Vénitiennes'.

The present building, by William Playfair, was opened in 1859. At that time the main interest of the general public was focussed on contemporary art (older paintings being seen mainly as works of reference and instruction for art students), and the principal acquisitions were of works by British painters, especially artists working in Scotland. By the 1890s public interest in the art of the past was beginning to gather momentum. It began with Rembrandt and other Dutch artists, whose

Titian, Diana and Actaeon *(Duke of Sutherland loan)*

work had a recognisable affinity with the earthy realism of the Glasgow school and their contemporaries. Rembrandt's 'Woman in Bed' and three Frans Hals portraits were presented around this time, and Vermeer's 'Christ in the house of Mary and Martha' not much later, in 1927.

The most significant changes came in 1903, with the beginning of a regular purchase grant from HM Treasury (then set at £1,000 a year), and in 1907 with the appointment of the first full-time professional curator. In 1919 a large capital sum was left to the Gallery by a Scottish businessman who had worked in Rotherham, James Cowan Smith. This allowed for the first time purchases of real significance like Turner's 'Somer Hill', Constable's 'Dedham Vale' and Chardin's 'Vase of Flowers'. The Government purchase grant was not increased until 1952, when it was raised to £2,500; by 1980 it had reached £80,000. With extra Treasury grants, works accepted in lieu

of estate duty and valuable help from the National Art Collections Fund, the Gallery has been able to acquire paintings of international importance, starting with the Velasquez 'Old Woman Cooking Eggs' in 1955, and including major works by El Greco, Gainsborough, Rubens, Elsheimer, Andrea del Sarto, Gerard David, Claude, Quentin Matsys, Seurat and Verrocchio. Among recent additions are an interior with a family group by the Danish neo-classical painter Baerentzen (a shrewd purchase), and Bernini's bust of Cardinal dal Pozzo.

Two long-term loans are of outstanding importance. The first of these is the two panels from the Trinity Altarpiece, painted in the 1470s by the Flemish artist Hugo van der Goes for the Chapel of the Holy Trinity in Edinburgh, which have been on loan from the Royal Collection since 1912. The other is a group of 26 paintings that have been on loan from the Duke of Sutherland since 1946, which in-

John Constable, Vale of Dedham, *1828*

clude Titian's 'Three Ages of Man', 'Diana and Actaeon' and 'Diana and Calisto', the seven pictures of the Sacraments by Poussin, Raphael's 'Holy Family with a Palm Tree' (recently cleaned) and his 'Bridgewater Madonna', Tintoretto's 'Deposition of Christ', and a Rembrandt self-portrait.

Outstanding gifts of pictures in this century have included the Vaughan Bequest in 1901 of 38 Turner watercolours (which may only be shown in January to save them from fading); the family pictures of Mrs Nisbet Hamilton Ogilvy in 1920; and two great gifts of French Impressionists and Post-Impressionists, one made by the Edinburgh advocate Sir Alexander Maitland in 1960, and the other the Richmond-Traill Collection, given by Isabel Traill in memory of her uncle Sir John Richmond in 1979.

Over the years Playfair's original building has been substantially modified, with first floor galleries added at both ends of the building, and a New Wing at a lower level, which looks out onto Waverley Station and is used for showing the main collection of Scottish painting. The Gallery was refurbished

Gauguin, The Vision of the sermon, *1888*

in 1988, when the last of the structural accretions of the 1930s were removed and the rooms carpeted to great advantage. At the same time the eight octagonal rooms on the main floor were rearranged, the walls hung with crimson felt throughout, furniture introduced, and the pictures hung one above the other, sometimes three deep (colour plate 9).

Until this rearrangement, the Gallery had been essentially a machine for looking at paintings, hung whenever practical at eye-level, with wall fabrics, reflections and other visual 'noise' re-

duced to a minimum. The overall impression was sacrificed to the focus on individual paintings. It is now a grand and impressive interior, a venue for splendid receptions and a feast for the eye of the casual visitor. The pictures (instinctively one calls them pictures rather than paintings) take their places as part of the decorative scheme.

Some of them thrive in this setting, perhaps none more so than Benjamin West's 'Alexander saved from a stag'. But West's picture is a vast, ranting melodrama, whereas the Gallery is a treasure house of international masterpieces, which connoisseurs are inclined to compare with the Frick Collection in New York and the art gallery in Dresden. These now have to take their chance. The masterly handling of the head in Lawrence's portrait of Lady Manners is lost to view, whilst Saenredam's marvellous church interior gains by extra height, but its cool, subtle colours are engulfed in a sea of burgundy. On the other hand, the big Rubens 'Feast of Herod' and the big Claude landscape are improved out of recognition.

But these are details, and the visitor is invited not to look at details but to absorb the whole brilliant effect. Some people, perhaps a minority, feel that it is a poor use of so many masterpieces. For many others it has been a fairy transformation scene. It will have been justified if the net effect over the next decade or so is 'to diffuse more widely in society a taste for the fine arts', as the members of the original Royal Institution wished.

Besides a regular bulletin on the activities of all three Galleries (including the **Gallery of Modern Art** and the **Portrait Gallery**), recent publications include a booklet on the building itself, a series of very brief monographs on a number of Scottish artists and catalogues of temporary exhibitions. A spacious room at one end of the building is reserved for exhibitions drawn from the Gallery's collection of old master prints and drawings, which is the most important in Scotland. Other exhibitions, except during the Edinburgh International Festival, are restricted mainly to Scottish themes.

David Wilkie, Pitlessie Fair, *1804 (detail)*

Royal Museum of Scotland, Chambers Street

Chambers Street, Edinburgh
EH1 1JF   (031) 225 7534
Open daily. Major building repairs
may necessitate closure of some
galleries – check with museum in
advance if you want to see
something specific. F ▣ & W
🏛 & 🚻 preferably book in
advance.

The two main buildings of the National Museum of Scotland are now under
a single Board and Director. Both are
called Royal Museum of Scotland, and
are distinguished only by their locations – Chambers Street and **Queen
Street**.

The Chambers Street Museum is
the former Royal Scottish Museum,
one of the two largest museum buildings in Scotland (**Glasgow Art Gallery and Museum** being the other).
The main building dates from 1861,
designed by Francis Fowke. Its principal feature is a vast hall with a glass
roof, one of the splendours of Victorian
cast-iron architecture, with travertine
marble floor and fish-ponds introduced in 1971. The museum was one
of those born of the Great Exhibition
of 1851 and was at first known as the
Museum of Science and Art. But it
also incorporated the collection of the

The Bolton Hearse

The main hall

Natural History Museum of Edinburgh University, which was begun in
the 17th century.

Such is the extent of the collections
that a ground plan is essential: there is
a free leaflet, and the museum will be
producing a new guide. The museum's
remit covers the same ground as the
Science Museum in London, most of
the Victoria & Albert Museum, and
parts of the British Museum. Things of
Scottish origin are not given special
priority, except that the Museum takes
on a responsibility for saving items of
unique importance to Scotland and,
inevitably, they are of particular interest to Scots. The main divisions are
Natural History; Geology; Technology
and Science; the Decorative and Applied arts; and Archaeology outside
Britain.

Apart from the push-button models
of engines, surely mandatory in a science museum, highlights of the transport section are the marvellous Bolton
Hearse, a distinctly oriental-looking

vehicle that was in use near Hadding-
ton, East Lothian from 1783, and the
Wylam Dilly steam engine of 1813.
The first pneumatic tyre is here too,
made for a bicycle by its inventor John
Boyd Dunlop, a Scotsman working in
Ireland.

In the natural history section there
are things all children must see, like
the 78 ft skeleton of a blue whale that
was stranded on the beach at North
Berwick in 1830. There are elephants
and crocodiles, turtles and snakes (including a black grass snake that was
brought into Kirkcaldy in a banana
boat). The bird hall displays birds that
can be seen in Scotland (foreign birds
are shown on a balcony elsewhere).
There is also a big collection of fish.

An extensive Evolution Hall, created
in 1975, gives a fairly detailed account
of the present theory of evolution up to
the emergence of man. The argument
is dense, much of it in words, and
unless taken round by a guide the
ordinary visitor is likely to concentrate

on the more spectacular elements, such as the replica skeleton of the Dinosaur or the giant Grand Sloth.

Round the main hall at first floor level is a display of European art. Small displays of ceramics – Wedgwood, Meissen, Delft, English slipware, faience, majolica, Spanish lustreware – are delightful and give a very good idea of the range of pottery and porcelain. Probably less attractive to the ordinary visitor is the extensive display of silver, most of it English. The contrast between the sturdy Huguenot silver of the early 18th century and the ostentation of a silver-gilt tea service made for Napoleon is striking. This is one of the areas where the museum, very properly, functions as a conglomerate of displays, each of which appeals to people who have a special interest in it. [The silver was tarnishing and has now been replaced by a display of glass. Ed.]

Off the balcony is a general collection of European sculpture and applied art from about 1200 to 1800. This ranges from a 16th century German carved and painted altarpiece to a case full of snuff boxes. A special case is reserved for the splendid Lennoxlove toilet service, made in 17th century France probably for the Duchess of Richmond and Lennox, and acquired for the museum in 1954. The light levels here are very low, and seem even more so after the brilliant main hall. Low levels are essential for preservation of tapestries, but not for the fine brass dishes and beautiful Limoges enamels, or items in silver, bronze and ivory. This tends to detract from the excellent plan of showing these things together; perhaps some compromise will eventually be found.

The Egyptian section has a striking series of mummies from different periods and some very sophisticated low reliefs, especially one of King Akhnaton. A good collection of Oriental art on the second floor has some interesting early tomb figures, and there are quite detailed explanations of the Chinese potters and their methods. Here and elsewhere people may regret a dearth of information on when or how the objects came to the museum, whether for instance as bequests of

important private collections in Scotland or individually by purchase.

Mixed in with the more permanent displays are exhibits that keep abreast with current interests. In the autumn of 1988, for example, the natural history section had a good display on taxidermy (an example of museums meeting the public interest of what goes on behind the scenes), and another on the exploitation of natural phenomena (in this case shells) and the problem of preventing species from becoming extinct. These are essentially displays with a short life, of the kind that one hopes will be toured to museums in other parts of Scotland. They represent what the visitor often has too little opportunity to realise in going round more permanent displays – the continuous research that goes on in a museum of this kind into the subjects represented in its collections.

A hall on the ground floor is reserved for a programme of larger temporary exhibitions. It is worth keeping an eye, too, on the activities of the education department. Their 'Discovery room' (which has recently been on

tour to Inverness and elsewhere) and a number of their small temporary exhibitions have been of great interest, and are by no means aimed exclusively at young people.

If these notes give a general impression of disorganisation, there is unfortunately good reason for this. In 1987 the building was found to be in a disastrous state of repair, in some places dangerous. Major restoration work had to begin with the roof of the main hall, which is now completed, but work on the roof will continue until 1992. At the end of 1988 a number of the main displays on the second floor, like ethnography and the rich geological collection in the Mineral Hall, were either closed or awaiting closure. (The agates are a major attraction, about which a booklet will soon be available, and the nucleus of the fossil display was collected by Hugh Miller, the Cromarty stonemason.) 1989 saw the beginning of work to refurbish six of the galleries, but this will continue into 1990 and beyond. Check with the museum in advance if you wish to see something in particular.

Skeleton from a 78ft long Blue Whale, collected in North Berwick, 1831

Royal Museum of Scotland, Queen Street

1 Queen Street, Edinburgh EH2 1JD
(031) 225 7534
Open daily. **F** &**W**
& preferably book in advance.

This is the former National Museum of Antiquities of Scotland. It has been housed in the same building as the **Scottish National Portrait Gallery** since it was built, entered by a doorway on the left of the entrance hall. The museum has however a much older history as the collection of the Edinburgh Society of Antiquaries, which was formed largely under the inspiration of the Earl of Buchan in 1780.

The collection is entirely of things Scottish or things brought to Scotland and found here in archaeological excavations. The displays – at least the displays that are best designed to reach the non-specialist – are mainly on the ground floor. After passing a case housing the bronze bowls from Helms-

12th century bell shrine from Argyllshire

dale in Caithness, the visitor enters a large area divided into bays, with windows like those of the **Portrait Gallery** now perforce blacked out for the protection of the exhibits. Each of the bays is devoted to a particular aspect of history or type of object. The objects themselves are carefully laid out in cases, and are clearly and mostly unobtrusively described. It is a work of thorough scholarship and methodical presentation. It is sad, since so many of these things are on show precisely because of their ancient splendour, that the scholarship is not matched by a corresponding visual sense in their display.

Here we see, in a short compass, a crowded room of sculptured Pictish stones and casts of stones; some beautiful carved woodwork, in particular from churches; some guns of superb craftsmanship in the section on warfare; and a surprising variety of bagpipes going back to the 18th century. The display of Scottish silver includes a very handsome communion cup and plate, the remarkable Galloway mazer, a good reconstruction of a silversmith's workshop, the Holyrood monstrance, and then – looking rather isolated, but with the commendable intention of bringing the display up to date – three pieces by a young silversmith now working in Edinburgh (this last being no doubt subject to periodic change).

A section on law and order is dominated by the 'maiden', the guillotine installed in Edinburgh in 1564 and long one of the favourites of younger visitors to the museum. A few costumes are shown in set pieces. In spite of the finery of an embroidered silk Court dress of the 1760s with a preposterously wide skirt, it is three figures in drab peasant clothing recovered from peat bogs in Caithness, Lewis and Shetland, that are for me the most evocative.

The first floor gallery survives in its original form as an open space. Here the ordinary visitor may well feel confused by the profuse array of flints, axe-heads, urns and other evidence essential to the study of archaeology. But there are occasional brilliant trea-

The 'Maiden'

sures from Norse, Pictish and Celtic times (ill. on cover), brought here from excavations all over the Scottish mainland and islands. These are likely to be the only exhibits for which, as a person of the 20th century, he can hope to feel much human contact.

Distinguished amongst them are a beautiful beaten bronze boar's head from Banffshire, perhaps of the 2nd century AD; a 'chamfrein', or animal-head mask, from Kirkcudbrightshire (which was wrongly interpreted and assembled when it was found in the 1820s and presented to Walter Scott); the elaborate silver-gilt Hunterston Brooch of the 7th century AD from Ayrshire, with inset amber and panels of gold wire; and the largest Norse hoard so far discovered, which comes from Sandwick in Orkney. Finally there is the St Ninian's Treasure, which is referred to under the **Shetland Museum, Lerwick**. This is unquestionably one of the most romantic and dramatic of all Scottish archaeological finds, made as recently as the 1950s. The real objects (colour plate 10) are entirely different to look at from the replicas in Lerwick, and hold a real sense of their quality and antiquity. But here visitors must use their imagination, for the way in which they are shown makes it difficult to appreciate their quality as works of art. An excellent booklet that is available on the Treasure does not atone for this.

The second floor has a display on Roman Scotland. This is dominated by things that were dug up at Newstead, near Melrose, one of the strongpoints in the Antonine Wall, which the Romans named Trimontium after the Eildon Hills. The finds, excavated before the First World War, are truly remarkable: cavalry helmets and face masks in beaten bronze, amphorae, cartwheels, decorated pottery hunt cups, two beautiful bronze jugs and much else besides. Another fruitful site was the fortress of Traprain Law, near Had-

dington. From Traprain Law came a hoard of late Roman silverware dug up in 1919: bowls, flagons, dishes – precious remains, distinguished for their craftsmanship although surely not for their beauty of shape.

In the end the impression persists of a museum in a kind of suspended animation between the old museum world and the new: between collections assembled centrally, classified according to types of artefact and preserved for examination by specialists, in which the Museum of Antiquities has had a long and honourable record, and the very different form of display that is needed to stir the imagination of the ordinary visitor, which can no doubt conflict with the needs of the archaeologist or antiquarian.

The building immediately opposite on Queen Street is also used by the museum. Temporary exhibitions have been shown there in the past, most notably the Celtic exhibition of 1985, 'Symbols of Power'. The publications available, apart from catalogues of special exhibitions and the booklet on the St Ninian's Treasure, tend to belong to the old museum world rather than the new.

Scottish National Gallery of Modern Art

Belford Road, Edinburgh EH4 3DR
(031) 556 8921
Open daily. ⬛ ⬛ ⬛   ⬛ W
⬛ & ⬛ contact Education Dept., National Galleries of Scotland

Collecting modern art has had a curious history in Britain since the middle of last century. At that time the collecting of modern paintings, especially of the British school, was accepted not only as a function of the **National Gallery** on the Mound but as its principal function. As time went on, popular enthusiasm for modern art gradually declined as artists' work became more difficult to appreciate readily, whilst older paintings came to be seen as objects of beauty and interest in themselves rather than as quaint survivals from the past whose main use was for training art students and for demonstrating how much art had advanced.

There then grew up a belief, which had no basis in fact, that the **National Gallery** was not permitted by statute to collect the work of living artists (the same myth also grew up round the National Gallery in London), with the result that for half a century, while other countries were collecting modern art, Scotland lagged behind. The situation was not put right until 1960, when the Regius Keeper's residence in Edinburgh's Royal Botanic Garden was converted for use as a gallery of modern art. It was of course far too small, and there were cries of woe from those who believed that accepting it as a temporary solution would kill off the chance of getting larger premises later.

In the event, the gallery proved enormously popular. More important, it justified the provision of an annual Government purchase grant, and although this was discouragingly small compared with the prices that the 'old masters' of modern art like Picasso and Matisse were than commanding, it was used with great effect over the following 20 years. A distinguishing feature

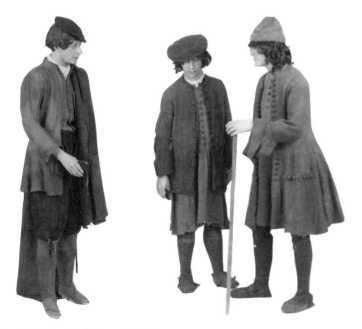

Woollen clothing, late 17th to mid-18th century

of the collecting policy was the representation of early 20th century masters like Kirchner, Nolde, Jawlensky and Derain, whose prices had not yet come to match the quality of much of their work. This meant that by 1980, when the possibility of taking over the present building was being considered, the importance of the collection and the esteem in which the gallery had come to be held were important factors in the Secretary of State's decision.

The Gallery was built as a school in 1828. Its attractions as a gallery were the severe lines of its classical façade behind an extensive area of lawn, sympathetic to the art of this century, and the internal layout with its wide stone-flagged corridors and rooms opening off them, even if many of the rooms themselves are small by museum standards.

More cries of woe, no doubt from many of the same people as before, who had meanwhile grown to love the gallery in the Botanic Garden, and who were convinced that the new site was too isolated. Again, the Jeremiahs were proved wrong. The conversion was imaginatively completed with a lively flicker of post-modernism in some of the detailing. This immediately lent the building a friendly atmosphere, an effect that could not have been predicted. The restaurant quickly established itself as a place of pilgrimage in its own right, and the car park completed the essential desiderata for a successful tourist attraction, which it has remained ever since.

Steven Campbell, Elegant Gestures of the Drowned after Max Ernst, *1986*

Jacob Epstein, Consummatum est, *1936–37*

The function of the collection is clear: that it should represent international art of this century, thus taking over where the **National Gallery** leaves off. The restricted scale of the rooms in both its former and present buildings have lent the gallery a character that is stable and almost domestic. This has been assisted by the fact that so much of the art of the first half of this century was on a domestic scale. Scottish painting has an honoured place, with excellent representation of work by Peploe, Gillies, Maxwell, Eardley, Redpath and Philipson, for example.

There have been shocks for press and public of the predictable kind from some of the acquisitions (and of course their cost), like the loathsome 'Nude girl on a fur' of 1932 by Otto Dix, or the junk sculpture of compressed motor cars by César, or the superrealism of John de Andrea's 'Model in repose', or the pop image of Roy Lichtenstein's 'In the car' (ill. on cover). But the Gallery absorbs these easily into its total image, partly because if you react strongly to any of them, there will be something of a totally different kind nearby that may suit your concept of art better.

Sculpture includes Epstein's impressive alabaster dead Christ, 'Consummatum est'; Giacometti's 'Woman with her throat cut'; figures by Henry Moore, Ernst Barlach and Marino Marini; and a group by Barbara Hepworth. Some are on the lawn in front of the building, and there are plans for a sculpture garden at the back, seen from the restaurant windows.

Since its foundation, the Gallery has received some important gifts, especially of the work of Scottish artists. Most notable are the Scott-Hay and Dr Lillie bequests, and the recent George and Isobel Neillands gift. Recent purchases have included work by Lucian Freud, Tinguely, Mark Boyle, Paolozzi, Philipson, Alan Davie, Fernand Léger's 'Les Constructeurs', Duchamp's 'Suitcase', and a range of work by younger Scottish painters like Bellany, Campbell, Wiszniewski and Currie.

There is a particularly good and comprehensive series of artists' prints which is rapidly growing (another practical way of representing artists whose paintings were beyond the Gallery's means). These can be consulted – a catalogue and up-to-date lists are available – and the prints are also drawn on for temporary exhibitions in the downstairs corridor that are changed about every three months. Temporary loan exhibitions are sometimes held, often timed to coincide with the Edinburgh International Festival, like 'The vigorous imagination' (of work by younger Scottish artists) in 1987 and 'Lucian Freud' in 1988.

The Gallery shares with the **National** and **Portrait Galleries** in their periodic bulletins. Publications, of importance for Scottish art of this century in particular, accompany the major temporary exhibitions. A catalogue of the permanent collection is available.

Scottish National Portrait Gallery

1 Queen Street, Edinburgh EH2 1JD
(031) 556 8921
Open daily. ▣ ⬤ W
⬤ & ⬤ contact Education Dept.,
National Galleries of Scotland

Although the desire to collect likenesses of the famous is one of the oldest motives for forming a museum, the portrait galleries in Edinburgh, London and Washington are in fact the only three national institutions that were formed solely for this purpose. Thomas Carlyle's view was that nothing brought history to life so vividly as to stand face to face with the images of the people who had made it. Another 19th century view was that the visitor would be encouraged to greater industry and moral rectitude if he gazed upon the likenesses of great men renowned for these virtues. This view is now mercifully forgotten, and Carlyle's begins to look rather marginal the more history comes to be understood

Thomas Gainsborough, 4th Duke of Argyll

as the history of ordinary people. Yet now more than ever, no one will dispute the value of collecting reliable likenesses of well-known, influential, or indeed characteristic 'ordinary' people, whatever criteria you care to apply.

The building, designed by Rowand Anderson and largely funded by John Ritchie Findlay of *The Scotsman*, was opened to the public in 1889. Bursting impudently out of the restrained Georgian façade of Queen Street, in flamboyant red sandstone bristling with statues, crockets and pinnacles, it proclaimed stridently the veneration of the late 19th century for the nation's past – at least in principle. In fact the enthusiasm was limited to representing, or rather symbolising, the past in modern terms. While, therefore, there was ample reference to the past in the architect's programme, with (modern) sculptures on the outside and (modern) murals within, very little wall space was conceded between the extensive windows to accommodate the historical portraits that the gallery was intended to display. This fundamental defect was finally overcome in the past six years or so by blocking out the windows almost completely, which only became a practical possibility with modern museum lighting. The displays are on three floors, and the infirm should note the location of the lift, which is actually inside the doorway to the other half of the building.

The original aim of the permanent collection was to represent Scotland's famous men and women. Much of this aim has already been realised, and it remains in the forefront of the Gallery's acquisitions policy. The display was traditionally chronological, with the earliest portraits on the ground floor and the Raeburn portraits in the big centre room at the top. [From spring 1990 the ground floor will be given over to joint displays with the **Royal Museum of Scotland**. Ed.]

Among the great and the good, most people will have their own favourites and their own dislikes. In a big collection of this kind, where comparatively little of it can be on show at one time, it is worth noting that complete lists are readily available to verify whether portraits of minor figures of particular interest to you are included, or indeed where they can be seen.

As works of art, certain portraits stand out: Gainsborough's 4th Duke of Argyll; Mytens' 1st Duke of Hamilton; Eworth's Lord Darnley; Richard Wilson's charming Flora Macdonald; Nasmyth's Robert Burns; Dobson's Charles Prince of Wales; groups and conversation pictures by Nasmyth and David Allan; the baptism of Bonnie Prince Charlie and the wedding of his parents; the composite picture of the execution of Charles I; the diminutive bronze bust of Mary Queen of Scots by Ponce Jacquio. Among portraits by Raeburn is James Hutton, a haunting image of the retiring scholar (even if the chairback grows out of his armpit). Sir Alexander Morrison was painted by his patient Richard Dadd in Bedlam in 1852.

Some of the portraits are on loan, meanwhile the Gallery pursues a very active policy of new acquisitions. This has recently come to include a vigorous and extremely imaginative series of specially commissioned portraits of influential Scots, from the Queen Mother to the miners' leader Mick McGahey, by established artists who are not established portrait painters and tend therefore to bring a fresh eye to the task.

While the Gallery remains the primary centre for portraits and records of portraits of well-known Scots, its remit has been gradually broadened in response to changing needs. A particular characteristic of the gallery has for some time been the temporary exhibitions of paintings and prints mounted each summer, not only on Scottish portraits or Scottish people, but on Scottish historical themes generally. One of the most recent was also one of the most popular, in celebration of Mary Queen of Scots. These exhibitions have also been the occasions for producing a continuous series of publications of a consistently high standard of scholarship, which must stand as one of the major contributions of the Gallery and its staff to the knowledge and understanding of Scotland. They

David Mytens, 1st Duke of Hamilton, *1629*

now include an excellent history of the building and early years of the Gallery itself, 'A Portrait Gallery for Scotland'.

Added to this is an important archive of visual evidence about Scottish dress and other aspects of social history, the Social History Index, not normally on display but always open to enquirers and increasingly used as a primary source of information.

Since 1928 the Gallery has held one of the main collections of the pioneering 19th century photographs of Hill and Adamson, which were mainly portraits, and this had established it as a centre for the study of early Scottish photography. With a new, wider emphasis on visual evidence about Scotland rather than solely the likenesses of great people, it was the natural base for a Scottish Photographic Archive, which was established in 1983. The Archive is committed to recording existing collections of photographs in Scotland; meanwhile the base collection has already been enriched by some extremely important and valuable gifts. Part of the exhibition space is now regularly reserved for displays of photographs, usually drawn from the permanent collection.

Alexander Nasmyth, Lady Mary McQueen Honyman with her children, *c.1795*

Scottish United Services Museum

Hospital Square, The Castle,
Edinburgh EH1 2NG
(031) 225 7534
Open daily. 🚇 to Edinburgh
Castle.   ♿ W
♿ & 🚻 welcome but must book in
advance.

Regimental museums are concerned primarily with the history of their respective regiments, often a celebration of historic triumphs on the field of battle and of the reputation won by them for their members. They are also in part the keepers of the regimental regalia, insignia and trophies, and often the medals of some of their most illustrious members; and they are in part the recorders of the regiment's most notable engagements. Their origins are to be found in the fierce pride and loyalty engendered in and after the 1914–18 war, and they serve to keep alive this spirit, on which the mettle of the regiments has always depended.

The Scottish United Services Museum is a branch of the National Museums of Scotland, and it is different in kind from the regimental museums (one of which, the *Royal Scots Museum*, is also within Edinburgh Castle). As the national museum, it houses the national collection of material relating to the Scottish armed forces. What is not so clearly established is the function of the displays that are mounted there for the general public: whether they should serve, in the absence of a war museum in Scotland, to record historic battles, or rather the way in which the regular and volunteer armed services in Scotland have developed.

At present the museum, engagingly introduced by two wooden Highland sentries presenting arms, offers two recently mounted displays. The main one is called 'The Story of the Scottish Soldier 1600–1914', and aims to tell us 'who these soldiers were, where they fought and what they achieved'. It is the story 'of suffering and destruction as well as of remarkable deeds of courage.' The story itself does indeed contain these things. So too does a lively,

Highlanders from the Crimean war

well-illustrated booklet that accompanies the exhibition, which ends with a revealing comparison of the characteristics and treatment of the Scottish footsoldier between 1680 and 1910.

The exhibition itself has a rather different emphasis. Display panels offer sufficient background information on the way the armed forces developed, judiciously illustrated with reproductions of contemporary prints and paintings. Most of the exhibits are in half-height showcases which run continuously round the outer walls, with space in the centre for full-length figures, occasionally grouped in small tableaux. The low-level lighting, the asthmatic roar of the air-conditioning, the carpet underfoot, the specially-designed showcases and the elegantly-printed labelling all proclaim a national museum, its responsibilities and its resources.

The story begins with the helmets of the 17th century. It is soon dominated by the Jacobite rebellion of 1745 and the Battle of Culloden, with its hideous claymores and pikes and halberds. It goes on to the 6,000 Scots who fought at Waterloo in 1815, the Crimea, and finally the state of the armed forces in August 1914, 'better trained, better equipped and better led than any of its predecessors'. In all this we get a fairly

Drum of Brigadier Henry Middleton's Regiment, c.1720

clear idea – largely through the printed texts – of the soldier's reputation at different periods and the changing role of the volunteer forces.

The actual objects on display, however, are to a large extent a parade of military dress. This is in itself fascinating, and must indeed represent a major part of the collections of the museum. We see the extraordinary variations in headdress, from the curious mitre of the 18th century and the shako that followed it. We see the touching little tunic worn by a boy bugler in the 1860s. We see the eternal ingenuity of the male in inventing new embellishments for himself. The ceremonial is all here, including those presentation swords which seem to share with tattooing a complete immunity from the common rules of visual good sense.

Somehow what is absent is a sense of the squalor and the cruelty: the king's shilling, the suppression of the Jacobites, the use of the armed forces to preserve law and order in times of peace, and the horrors of the Crimea. (We are not told about army welfare until the 1820s, when it began to be taken seriously.) The story is well told but, partly because of the nature of what can be shown in a museum, and perhaps also because of some of the same sense of pride and loyalty that pervades the regimental museums, it is a rather one-sided account.

The second exhibition is devoted to a history of the military band. The instruments involved are often unexpected, from bassoons and trombones to the curious 18th century serpent. Their varied and beautiful shapes lend themselves to a lively formal display. Then there are surprises in the story (which is well told), for instance that the bagpipe was not officially recognised until 1854, or the revelations about the dangerous role of the bandsman in battle and its effect on the design of his uniform. Above all there is the element of pomp and circumstance, judiciously continued into the underlying colour scheme of crimson, royal blue and gold. The presentation is completed by a discreet tape of different kinds of military music.

ELGIN (G)

Elgin Museum

1 High Street, Elgin, Moray
IV30 1EQ   (0343) 543675
Closed until 1990 for complete overhaul of museum. Thereafter closed October to March, and otherwise closed on Sundays (seasonal closure subject to review). ▣
♿ but no disabled access to upper gallery.

In the early part of the 19th century a number of scientific and philosophical societies were founded in different parts of Scotland. The Elgin and Morayshire Literary and Scientific Association, formed in 1836, is not the earliest (that distinction probably goes to Perth), nor is the building, which was completed in 1843, the earliest of those that were specially designed to house museum collections. Nevertheless the museum holds a place of special importance as it is one of three that are furthest to the north (the other two being at **Inverness** and **Forres**), and is the only one that has retained its independence rather than being absorbed by the local authority. In fact its founding body, the Moray Society as it is now called, recently launched a successful appeal for funds to restore the old building and to reconstitute the facilities for storing and displaying the collection. At the time of writing, the museum is closed and the collection stored away to allow for complete overhaul from the roof downwards. [Scheduled to reopen 1990. Ed.]

The building is of the standard early museum design, with a single large space lit by a central skylight and a gallery running round it at first floor level. Others of this type are at **Montrose** and **Forres**. The interior is very attractive and is certainly the most elegant of the three, though the façade is not so distinguished to look at.

The three prime movers of the Elgin Society included the Minister, Revd Dr George Gordon, and the Town

Crouched mummy burial from Lake Titicaca

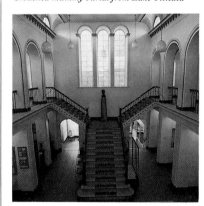

Interior view of Elgin Museum

Clerk Patrick Duff, who published a book on the geology of Moray six years later. They were men of their time, characteristic of the beginning of Victoria's reign, with a wide ranging intellectual curiosity combined with an intense desire to explore the antiquarian and naturalist aspects of their own region.

Moray offered a rich field for the exploration of fossil remains because of the nature of its geological formation. Some of the fossils found were recognised to have an international significance – one of the key questions was the incidence of reptiles – and in 1877 Thomas Huxley, one of the foremost scholars in the field, published an account of the crocodilian remains found in the Elgin sandstones. The Elgin fossil fish and reptiles include a number that are unique, most famous of which is the skull known as the *Elginia Mirabilis*. Perhaps more evocative for those of us who are not expert in the field are the footprints left by these creatures in the sands of two or three hundred million years ago, especially when they have between them marks made by the creature's tail as it dragged along behind.

But the Literary and Scientific Society was also concerned – like its sisters elsewhere in Scotland – with evidence of life outside the Moray region, and the museum still retains evidence of this in its collections. Young visitors tend to react most immediately to the shrunken head from Equador or the head-hunter's basket decorated with monkey skulls. More unusual still is the crouched mummy of a kind that was common in Peru up to the demise of the Incas in the 16th century. It was found in a cave on the Isle of Maretasse in Lake Titicaca, high up in the Andes, by a man from the Black Isle called James Fletcher, who gave it to the Elgin Society in 1846 (there was as yet no museum at Inverness). Preserved in a specially made glass case, grinning hideously now that the flesh has withered away, she was supposed to have been a princess.

There are sculptures brought back from India in 1852, but also stone sculptures from nearby, including two lifesize 17th century 'savages' that used to stand sentinel at the entrance gate of Thunderton House, once an important residence in Elgin. The crown of the archaeological collection is the Pictish stone carving of a bull, one of six found at Burghead, a few miles to the north west on the coast.

Further displays describe the changes in the land of Moray up to the last century, including agriculture and a notable exhibit, the sole-surviving 18th century leather boat, the Spey Currach. [Items spanning the history of Elgin itself will also be shown. Ed.]

EYEMOUTH (B)

Eyemouth Museum

Auld Kirk, Market Place, Eyemouth,
Berwickshire TD14 5HE
(08907) 50678
Closed November to Easter, & on Sunday mornings Easter to July and September to November. 🔊
♿: exhibition area upstairs not accessible to wheelchairs.
🎨 & 🍴 must book in advance; reduced charge.

No visitor to Eyemouth fails to realise that it is still an active fishing port, and no intelligent visitor should leave without learning about the terrible tragedy that overtook the fishing community there in 1881 and completely overshadowed their lives for a long time. And the place to learn about it is in the Eyemouth Museum.

The museum was brought into being in 1981 to mark the centenary of the disaster. The late Georgian church in the centre of the town, the Auld Kirk, was sold for the nominal sum of £1 to a Trust that was formed by Berwickshire District Council, and the Borders Region took a lease from the Trust for an area that is used as the Tourist Information Centre.

The Tourist Centre leads straight into the museum. The visitor is taken through a fairly tight maze, which is constructed unpretentiously with common tubular scaffolding under the black painted vault of the old church interior. The route takes him through an engaging clutter of the fisherman's trade, the nets, baskets and lines, which act as a setting for a series of small displays, each representing one of the particular activities or concerns of Eyemouth and its people. It is a little like listening to an old resident of the town who has got so much to tell that he hardly has time to draw breath.

He is worth listening to. Eyemouth has supported a number of country crafts as well as the fishing industry. So the displays are about fishing lures and hooks, about dairying and farming,

Wooden patterns for a waterwheel and cogs

about the trades of the wheelwright, the miller, the blacksmith and those more directly related to the fisheries: coopering, boat building, net and sail making, and the lifeboat. And there are sections on the local wildlife, and the window of a pharmacist's shop.

The displays gain from having avoided the current museum cliché of large screen-printed boards telling the story in bold type. Each section has been thoughtfully considered; the photographs illuminate the objects themselves, and these are numbered so that their brief descriptive notes can be grouped together to avoid clutter.

Another characteristic is that, rather than seeing reconstructions of a farm or a wheelwright's or cooper's shop, with the intention of giving a sense of its atmosphere, we are shown the tools that were used in these trades. On closer inspection like this many of them are seen as works of considerable craftsmanship or ingenuity in their own

Window of a pharmacist's shop

right: for instance a long cross-cut saw, a beam scale and a sack-lifting machine from a mill, wooden cogs for mill machinery and the patterns for making a water wheel.

Half way round are the bow and wheelhouse of 'Talisman III' with a recording that gives an account of boatbuilding in Eyemouth. Further on is a reconstruction of a fisherman's livingroom of the turn of the century.

But overshadowing it all is the story of the disastrous storm of Friday 14 October 1881. The day started treacherously with bright sunshine and a calm sea, but gave way to a hurricane all the way from Orkney to the English Channel, with its greatest fury unleashed on the east coast of Scotland. 189 men were lost from this small community, 129 of them from Eyemouth itself.

A long tapestry, sewn by volunteers, hangs at one end of the museum. It is strongly coloured, part realistic, part symbolic, and divided into a number of panels with lists of the boats and the men that were lost, most of them between 17 and their mid-thirties in age. In a case nearby are some pathetic relics of the disaster – mourning cards printed for two of the men, a watch found on one of the bodies, a tobacco tin washed up on the beach.

Upstairs is a small area used to show temporary exhibitions. There is a well-produced booklet on the museum and a good series of inexpensive leaflets, aimed mainly but not exclusively at young readers, on the various activities of Eyemouth people past and present, including the once flourishing trade of smuggling.

FORRES (G)

Falconer Museum

Tolbooth Street, Forres IV36 0PH
(0309) 73701
Closed Sundays (except during July and August when open Sunday afternoons), and closed Saturdays October to May. **F**
&: wheelchair access to ground floor only.
👫 & 👫 welcome but must book in advance.

The Falconer Museum is named after two natives of Forres. Alexander Falconer (1797–1856) was a merchant in Calcutta, who left £1,000 to establish 'a public museum for objects of art and science'. His brother Hugh (1808–65) was an eminent botanist and geologist, known particularly for his work on the fossil mammals of the Sewalik Hills in India. He also left money, and a collection of Sewalik fossils.

The museum building was completed in 1871. The interior follows the same pattern as those at Elgin and Montrose, the whole public area consisting of a central hall with a gallery round it, lit by a rooflight that runs

Hugh Falconer photographed c.1860

down its length. The ornamentation of the façade is significant. A head of Hugh Falconer is above the doorway, flanked above the windows by Isaac Newton and Baron Cuvier, representing the international authorities on Falconer's principal interests (five Scottish authorities gracing the win-

Showcase with funerary urn excavated at Findhorn in 1988

The museum building of 1871

FORT WILLIAM (H)

The West Highland Museum

Cameron Square, Fort William,
Inverness-shire PH33 6AJ
(0397) 2169
Closed Sundays. ⬛
&: inaccessible to wheelchairs;
long stairs.
⋔ & ⋔ small groups welcome;
schools must book.

dows down the side of the building include Walter Scott, Hugh Miller and James Watt). Baron Cuvier, who died in 1832, was however a confirmed opponent of the theories on evolution that were by then emerging, whilst Hugh Falconer was to become a friend of Charles Darwin's. By the time Cuvier's bust was being carved for the façade at Forres, Darwin's *Origin of Species* had been in print for 12 years.

On display in the museum are some of the fossil fish collected by Lady Eliza Maria Gordon Cumming between 1839 and 1842. Lady Cumming was a keen gardener and made her garden at Altyre famous. It is reported that during her fifteenth pregnancy she saved a woman's life by stopping a bolting horse, but died soon afterwards from her injuries. Her claim to fame, however, rests on her work as a pioneer in the study of fossil fish from the Old Red Sandstone, which she collected in the quarries at Lethen Bar, near Nairn. The Swiss naturalist, Louis Agassiz, came to see them and reproduced many of her drawings in his standard work on fossil fish. Her collection was for many years on loan to the museum from her descendants, but most of it was sold 15 years ago to the **Royal Museum of Scotland**.

Among objects that were in the museum collection from its early days

are a horse-shoe crab, a piece of table said to have been used by Mary Queen of Scots, a scaly anteater (there is another in **Nairn**), and a Maori skull, presented between 1868 and 1883. A singular, though presumably not unique, acquisition which may have come in by then is a chamberpot with a bust of Napoleon at the bottom of it, reputedly used at meetings of the Forres Trafalger Club from about 1815–40. (Did all towns in Britain, one wonders, have Trafalgar Clubs, and did they all share this elementary sense of humour?)

There is a case of local minerals, giving their locations (there were silver mines at Lossiemouth to the north). The work of Forres silversmiths is represented, and the natural history section displays birds found in the district. A very recent acquisition is a cordonned pottery urn of about 1500–2000 BC, one of the largest known, which contained the remains of a cremated young woman and child, excavated at Findhorn in 1988.

The museum has produced a good series of information sheets (11 so far) on the museum and its collections, and on things of interest in Moray Region, for instance geology and mineralogy, especially the Lecht iron-manganese mine, seven Moray women, and the blacksmiths at Tomintoul.

This museum grew out of one man's enthusiasm for the history of the area. He was Victor Hodgson of Onich, a few miles to the south of Fort William. Hodgson organised two loan exhibitions of things from private houses across the country; a number of the loans were made into gifts, and these formed the nucleus of a permanent collection. That was in 1922. Within three years the collection had grown to the extent that a home for it had become an urgent necessity. An appeal was launched and the old British Linen

The British Linen Bank building

Reconstruction of a 19th century croft house interior

clude a matchlock gun, reputedly the one that killed Colin Campbell of Glenure, R.L. Stevenson's 'Red Fox' in *Kidnapped*. There are early sporrans going back to the 17th century, and a distinguished collection of powder horns and flasks. More gruesome is a birching table, with holes for the culprit's wrists, which was in official use in Fort William as late as 1948.

At one stage the visitor suddenly comes upon a cool, bare, panelled room of the early 18th century, brought from the Governor's house in the old Fort William, which was demolished in 1936. Its combination of military severity and elegant architectural proportions is a striking contrast to the more ornate interiors we associate with the Queen Anne period. On the way upstairs is a reconstruction of the interior of a croft house. Seen through a window opening, the darkened room gives an impression that is probably very true to life.

The first floor contains principally relics associated with Bonnie Prince Charlie. Wall panels give a concise summary of the events of the 1745 rebellion and the Prince's life. There are Stuart and Jacobite medals, Jacobite wine glasses and snuff mulls of the period. A gift from Charles Hepburn (of Red Hackle Whisky) includes a

Bank building was acquired. Although Georgian, it is one of the oldest buildings in Fort William in the centre of the town.

Part of the character of the museum comes from the support it has received over the years from the more influential families in the West Highlands, which had objects of great interest, rarity and value to give, and have given generously. This attitude itself springs from a strong sense of loyalty to the Highlands and a respect for its past, which is highly coloured by its association with Bonnie Prince Charlie and the legends surrounding him. Even when at times the evidence for associating objects with him is tenuous, the strength of these legends is itself an essential component of the culture of the Highlands, and this is brought home vividly to the visitor.

Another part of the museum's character stems from the fact that from quite early days it has been in the charge of a professional curator. This has ensured a certain standard in the continuing care of the collections and their presentation, with clear arrange-

ment and helpful typewritten labels. And incidentally it also brings a certain historical detachment to bear on the traditional history of some of the objects on display.

Cases of armour and weapons are almost exclusively Scottish, and in-

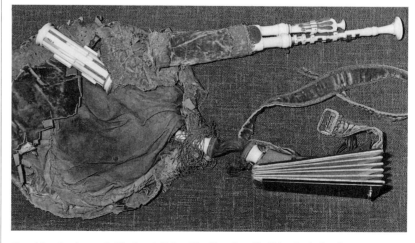

French bagpipes bequeathed by Bonnie Prince Charlie to the wife of his valet de chambre

sash reputedly the Prince's and cannon balls from Culloden. The most intriguing and popular item is the famous 'secret portrait' of the Prince, an apparently meaningless painting that becomes a portrait when reflected in a cylinder placed at its centre. It was found in a London shop by the museum's founder, Mr Hodgson. A quite recent acquisition is a set of French bagpipes that were bequeathed by Bonnie Prince Charlie to the wife of his *valet de chambre*, and bought by I. Skene of Rubislaw in Rome 14 years later, in 1802.

Also on this floor are important examples of early tartan dress, which are not only rare but extremely beautiful in colour, and include coats with short tails and waistcoats, and what is possibly the earliest surviving kilt, with box pleats, from the 18th century. Other things of interest are the Poltalloch harp, a 'clarsach' dating from the late 19th century; a Highland outfit given by Queen Victoria to her servant John Brown; geological samples from Glencoe and Ben Nevis; and a group of Highland brooches. Some of the brooches, as well as fossils and examples of tartan dress, were in the important Carmichael collection, now on loan to the museum from the collector's grandson.

There is a section on local birds and beasts, including the Scottish wild cat and the golden eagle. A section on industrial development gives an account of Telford's Caledonian Canal, including 'Neptune's staircase', the famous series of locks at Banavie just to the north of Fort William. It also includes an account of aluminium production from bauxite (there is a rolling-slab lump of aluminium from Lochaber weighing 1200 lbs), and a model of the ill-fated Wiggins Teape pulp mill at Fort William, work on which began under a government scheme in 1963 and which foundered through transport difficulties.

Finally it is difficult to resist a mention of the indomitable Henry Alexander, who successfully drove a Model T Ford to the top of Ben Nevis in 1911, celebrated here in a photograph taken on the way down.

GAIRLOCH (H)

Gairloch Heritage Museum

Auchtercairn, Gairloch, Ross-shire
(0445 83) 243
Closed October to Easter, otherwise closed Sundays. 🚻 ▣ 🅿
♿ W
♿ & ♿ welcome but must book in advance

Gairloch Heritage Museum stands at the entrance to the village as you come up the road from Achnasheen, with two sailing boats on the ground outside and a lighthouse just behind them. Its avowed purpose is to explain and interpret past life in the parish of Gairloch. If this seems a limited ambition, it must be borne in mind that the parish, although it counts only some 2,000 inhabitants, extends all the way from Loch Torridon in the south to Little Loch Broom in the north. The museum was made by converting parts of an old steading. It is an independent organisation staffed by local volunteers. The fact that this is still the case

11 years after the museum was first opened demonstrates the commitment of the people of Gairloch to the museum and their willingness to share their knowledge of the area with visitors.

Meanwhile the museum's reputation and the number of visitors to it have steadily increased, and gradually more buildings have been converted or added. A restuarant, converted from a barn in 1980, now stays open from 9.30am to 10pm serving a menu that includes local crab, prawns and wild salmon. More recently, an extension was built to house an archive of records of the parish, including tapes of oral accounts, many of them in Gaelic, which are being transcribed and translated.

The lantern and foghorn from the old lighthouse of 1910 at Rubha Reidh have just been added. The lantern is plainly visible in the glass section of a tower with a round roof which was specially built for it as an extension to the museum.

The two fishing boats on display outside the museum – ingeniously sunk into the ground so that we see them as if at water level – were both built locally. The larger of the two was built around 1910 in the open air at Alligin without mechanical equipment

Outside the museum, with the lantern from Rhuba Reidh lighthouse & fishing boat of c.1910

Very rare portable wooden pulpit

or preliminary drawings, the keel being laid by eye. It is 32 feet long, inspired by the 'Zulu' type of fishing boat developed at Lossiemouth in the 1880s, and it was manned by a crew of four.

Unattractive to look at but of special interest to the area is a lump of iron slag. Iron ore was found around Loch Maree and, together with the existence of extensive woods for making charcoal, made iron smelting a practical proposition. Furnaces were started about 1607. An Act of the Scots Parliament soon prohibited the cutting of timber for this purpose, in order to protect the environment, but by 1612 Sir George Hay had regained permission. Wrought and pig iron were exported to the south and abroad from three blast furnaces (the first in Scotland was at Poolewe) until the huge call on charcoal did indeed deplete the woods around the Loch.

Early archaeological finds from the area dating from 3,000 BC to 500 AD are set out individually in a showcase. Beside it is a Pictish symbol stone found at Strath, Gairloch, in 1948, which bears the common fish symbol that has been adopted as a 'logo' for the museum.

A recent addition is the grocery store of one F. MacRae, (colour plate 11), which was removed from a tin shed at Melvaig, on the road to the Rubha

Reidh lighthouse to the north of Gairloch. The shed is shown in a photograph of 1984.

Perhaps the rarest exhibit is a portable wooden pulpit. After the Disruption of the Scottish Church in 1843 these pulpits were used by the minister and precentor of the Free Presbyterian Church during open air communion ceremonies in the Highlands. (The practice was then far from new, and Defoe describes a tent–preaching to a congregation of nearly 7,000 on a steep hillside in Dumfriesshire in the 1720s, which lasted for almost seven hours.) This pulpit was in use at Shieldaig on the south of Loch Torridon between 1893 and 1920. A photograph, probably from the 1920s, shows the vast congregation at a tent–preaching of this kind at Plockton, a few miles to the south.

A recent extension is used to house temporary exhibitions. At other times it shows a historical review of the Highlands: the Picts, Celts and Gaels; St Columba and the coming of Christianity; the dominance of the Lord of the Isles in the early middle ages; and later life in the Highlands up to the time of the clearances. Illustrations of the more recent past are provided by a display of photographs, and there is an excellent series of leaflets, simply produced and cheap to buy, focussed not on particular items in the museum collection but on the distinctive features and activities of the area that they represent – the iron works, the lighthouse, the fishing boats, and so on.

Demonstration whisky still

GLASGOW (S)

The Burrell Collection

Pollok Country Park, 2060
Pollokshaws Road, Glasgow
G43 1AT   (041) 649 7151
Open daily. 🇫 📧 🅿 ♿ W
⚭ contact Friends Society
(GAGMA) for guided tours.
⚭ contact Glasgow Museums
Education Service (041) 334 1131/
649 9929

The approach to this museum is through Pollok Park, and the first impression is of a long building of pink sandstone and glass set among trees. The entrance is through the great 16th century doors and carved stone archway from Hornby Castle, Yorkshire, rebuilt into the modern masonry. The archway is one of several monumental features that Burrell bought late in his life from another great collection, that of his American contemporary, the newspaper owner William Randolph Hearst. It symbolises both the transatlantic flavour of Burrell's collection and the unusual integration of the building and its contents.

The main part of the interior is conceived as a single space, with white stone floors, light grey walls and tubular concrete pillars supporting a roof of glass and laminated timber. The space has been so contrived that there is a sense of continuity between the main areas, rather than of going through a series of doorways. Monotony is avoided by ingeniously retaining the contrasts between bright light, in places where it is helpful and permissible, and the low light level that is essential for instance for the rich collection of tapestries.

On the north side, where objects from ancient civilisations are displayed, the museum is built immediately up against woodland, and the entire wall along this side is glass down to floor level, with minimal dividers in light-coloured wood. So there is hardly any visual interruption between the immutable glazed earthenware Buddhist disciple on his pedestal and the trees outside that change with the seasons (colour plate 6). It was a stroke of genius.

The building and the collection are seen together, and are made to work together, the nature of the collection and even of individual objects dictating the arrangement of the rooms. And the way in which the objects are presented reflects the motives of the collector. Burrell saw everything – Roman helmets from the time of Christ, medieval stained glass, Degas' ballet dancers – as objects of aesthetic beauty in 20th century terms.

This concept of the past was extended, in Burrell's lifetime, to the house he lived in, Hutton Castle near Berwick-upon-Tweed. This was originally a border fortress, which Burrell bought in 1916 and remodelled extensively (with some not uncharacteristic arguments with the architects). The modern fittings of the rooms were carefully designed to harmonise with the antique furniture they were to accommodate. It was a condition of Burrell's will that the three principal rooms should be incorporated in the museum when it was built. This condition, which may have seemed restrictive when it was imposed, becomes more valuable the further away we

move from the aesthetic ideas that gave rise to this kind of interior decoration, with suits of armour standing guard over the guests in the drawing room.

The collection itself has particular strengths. There is a strong representation of North European medieval art, which was one of Burrell's enduring enthusiasms. This includes a superb range of medieval stained glass shown against the windows on the south side where its effect is unfortunately diminished by the light that comes in all round it. There is a rare collection of old tapestries and carpets, and of Oriental art. The paintings include several key 15th century works, for instance by Giovanni Bellini, Memling and Cranach, and a strong representation of 19th century French painters, Degas especially.

Much of the collection is displayed as it was bought, as unconnected items, especially the objects from ancient civilisations, and this encourages visitors to see them separately, and to have their own preferences and prejudices. They may choose the 12th century French enamelled copper-gilt châsse with the scene of the murder of Thomas à Becket, or the 17th century English stumpwork scene of Esther and Ahasuerus (with a charmingly lumpy city of towers in the background), or the Chinese model of a

Stained glass from St Denis, c.1140

storehouse about 2,000 years old, or Hogarth's portrait of Mrs Lloyd, or the monumental Renaissance archway at the entrance.

As a private collection it was vast, comprising over 8,000 items, and it is not by any means all on view at the same time. An area downstairs and a first floor section of the building are reserved for temporary displays from the collection itself, or relevant exhibitions brought in from outside.

Behind the collection and its building is the man himself although, interestingly, his is not such a vivid presence as that of William Hunter at the **Hunterian**. Sir William Burrell (1861–1958) was a Glasgow shipowner, brilliantly successful, reputedly fairly ruthless and not a little eccentric. He gave his collection and an endowment for building the gallery to the City of Glasgow in 1944, but there were protracted delays and the gallery was not opened until 1983. A full account of the man, his business flair, his tireless pursuit of beautiful things (always his personal choices), his inveterate penny-pinching, and the difficulties and delays before the museum was finally opened, is given by the first Keeper of the Collection, Richard Marks, in 'Burrell: A portrait of a collector'. It is one of several good publications that are available on the collection.

The hall from Hutton Castle rebuilt in the museum

Glasgow Art Gallery & Museum

Kelvingrove, Glasgow G3 8AG
(041) 357 3929
Open daily. 🇫 🖼 🅿
♿ W: wheelchair lift at front door.
👥 contact Friends society
(GAGMA) for guided tours.
👫 contact Museum Education
Service (041) 334 1131. ☀

Museums cannot be all things to all men, but Glasgow museums come near enough to being all things to all Glasgow people – perhaps especially to Glasgow children. This, the flagship of the City's museums, grew out of a great international exhibition held in Kelvingrove in 1888 to raise the funds for the museum project. By 1901 the magnificent pile of red sandstone was completed, now handed over to Glasgow Corporation by the originators of the scheme, and a second international exhibition was held round it in celebration.

The atmosphere of that time clings tenaciously to the stones of the museum – the air of prosperity and self-confidence of the business community, the staunch civic pride, the faith in Glasgow as the centre of the empire and the world, the moral certainties of culture and education. In a way, the collection of silver vases and trophies from Tiffany's and elsewhere, bequeathed by Sir Thomas Lipton, the grocer from Glasgow's east end, epitomises this.

Education meant the successful men of Glasgow providing the chance for younger men to follow them. And this sense accompanies you as soon as you enter the immense central hall of the biggest museum building in Scotland, with its continuous, confused hubbub rather like a big railway terminus. This is a place for everybody, not for the chosen few. There is an agreeable feeling that nothing will be too la-di-da, there will be a real concern for what is likely to interest the ordinary visitor, the coffee shop and restaurant will charge modestly, and however out-

landish the Egyptian mummy or the stuffed animals or the tomahawks, what is native to Scotland and Glasgow will never be far away.

So, in the natural history section, the narwhal's tusk and the embryo whales in bottles from South Georgia are here, side by side with a case of skins from endangered species confiscated by HM Customs and, closer to home, displays about hogweed and mushrooms (and their dangers) and about Scottish farm crops, with their end products indicated with beer cans and porridge packets. But you must expect to find that next time you come the displays will have been removed to make way for subjects of more topical interest.

In the fine art section, which is one of the main strengths of the museum, works are being acquired by Scottish painters as they become established – Alan Davie, William Gear, David Donaldson, Stephen Campbell and so on. Modern British sculpture – Caro, Paolozzi, Ian Hamilton Finlay – is here too, although it is ill at ease beside the coy naked ladies carved in white marble of a century before. 'Christ of St John of the Cross' by the Catalan surrealist Salvador Dali, bought from the artist's easel in 1952, remains a

Greenwich field armour for horse and rider, c.1550–60

Rembrandt, Man in Armour, *1655 (detail)*

curiously isolated phenomenon which has passed into Glasgow folklore. We are left with a sense of the good intention of keeping up, but without the assurance and conviction that greet us for instance in the art gallery in **Aberdeen** or in the small **Maclaurin Gallery** at Alloway.

Somehow that is not quite what the museum at Kelvingrove is about. Built into the head of the north stairway is a black bronze relief by Harry Bates of the blind Homer playing his harp to two scantily clad girls in listening attitudes. It was bought at the exhibition that raised the funds for the building in 1888, and it tells us a lot about the late Victorian understanding of Art, beauty and the classical world. The Glasgow school of painters, most of whom reacted sharply to this aesthetic, was in full flood at this time. They are well represented in the collection now, but mainly by works that were given later by the men who supported the artists in their lifetime. The tradition is kept alive, or at least revived, by a display devoted to Charles Rennie Mackintosh, including a partial reconstruction of one of the famous Cranston tearooms.

With older paintings the museum has always been on surer ground. The foundation was a collection that was particularly strong in early Italian art,

1 Right   16th century Italian spinet in a 17th century case. Dean Castle, Kilmarnock.

2 Below   Girl in a Boat by G. P. Chalmers (1833–78). McManus Galleries, Dundee (Orchar Collection).

3 *Opposite   Kirbuster, inside the 'firehoose'.
Orkney Farm & Folk Museum, Corrigall and
Kirbuster, Orkney.*

4 *Above   Wooden butcher's shop, 1880s.
Museum of Childhood, Edinburgh.*

5 *Left   Egyptian cat, 600–300 BC.
Anthropological Museum, Aberdeen.*

6   *Interior view of the galleries, north side. The Burrell Collection, Glasgow.*

7 Above   Royal Mail
coach, 1840. Museum of
Transport, Glasgow.

8 Right   Paisley shawl,
1855–65. Paisley Museum
and Art Gallery, Paisley.

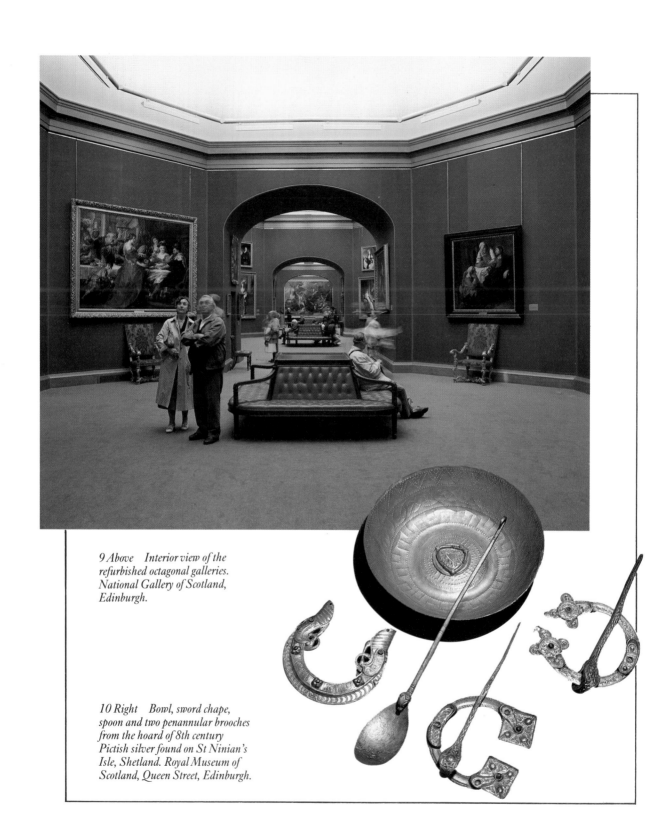

9 Above Interior view of the
refurbished octagonal galleries.
National Gallery of Scotland,
Edinburgh.

10 Right Bowl, sword chape,
spoon and two penannular brooches
from the hoard of 8th century
Pictish silver found on St Ninian's
Isle, Shetland. Royal Museum of
Scotland, Queen Street, Edinburgh.

11 *Interior of the grocery store of F. MacRae.*
Gairloch Heritage Museum, Gairloch.

*12 Tooth of a mastodon found in Ohio and sent to Hunter for identification,
with reconstruction drawings by Jan Van Rymsdyk. Hunterian Museum, Glasgow.*

including the 'Adultress before Christ' attributed to Giorgione. It was put together by a Glasgow coach-builder, Archibald McLellan, who died in 1854. (The galleries in Sauchiehall Street that housed his collection will be reopened as part of Glasgow Museums for important temporary exhibitions from 1990.) It is now Scotland's largest collection of old masters outside the **National Galleries**. It contains some major Dutch 17th century paintings, including Rembrandt's 'Young Man in Armour'; French paintings that range from the beautiful panel of a saint in armour with a donor by the Master of Moulins to a splendid group of Impressionists and Post-Impressionists; and a strong representation of Scottish art besides the Glasgow school.

Decorative arts, an important range of arms and armour, archaeology including things from Ancient Egypt . . . the list is as comprehensive as a national museum. I am tempted to dwell on the ethnographic display. It is a splendid collection and, until the **Royal Museum of Scotland** is back in business, it is one of two places in Scotland where we can see this range of exotic artefacts. The other is the exhibition in the **Anthropological Museum, Aberdeen**. Both displays are excellent, but the contrast between them is extremely interesting.

Typically, the exhibits were mostly collected in the last quarter of the 19th century when the Empire was at its height, sometimes under hazardous or irregular circumstances. They are restored and seen at their best, arranged in cases by their country of origin with simple, straightforward descriptions. There is no attempt here to evoke the environment in which these things were used, or to draw parallels between different cultural practices. It is fundamentally a museum display of the old kind. Yet it is hard to believe that anyone can fail to have their imagination fired by moving among these cases. It is a place for exciting discoveries you make on your own: things that challenge abruptly your idea of what is beautiful or artistic; unexpected ways of putting together natural materials, wood, leather, clay, straw, the primitive requirements of survival; and then in sudden contrast the highly sophisticated craftsmanship of the Indians and Chinese. These things are all eloquent of cultures distant from our own, which raise questions about things we take for granted in our own way of life.

People will find their own favourites – it's like window-shopping. For me it was the marvellous mask and the clubs and axes from Melanesia, the Ethiopian shield ornamented with fretted gold, a ceremonial axe from the Congo, the funerary screen from the Niger delta of three men with their betasselled fantasy hats, and the Ting Kia 'armour with nails' from China. These things in reality, even behind glass, are quite different from their shadows on a television screen.

There is a well stocked bookshop, which offers an attractive souvenir volume on the building and the collections with good illustrations.

[Considerable changes to displays are now under way in preparation for Glasgow's year as European City of Culture in 1990. Ed.]

Wooden funerary screen from Nigeria

Hunterian Art Gallery

University of Glasgow, 82 Hillhead Street, Glasgow G12 8QQ
(041) 330 5431
Closed Saturday afternoons and all day Sunday. ▉ (small ▉ for the Mackintosh House). ▉ W
▉ & ▉ welcome but must book in advance.

This is a recent building, completed in 1981, specially designed to house the paintings and drawings belonging to William Hunter and the art collection that has since been formed round them, which was hitherto housed in the **Hunterian Museum** in the main university building across the road with the rest of Hunter's collection. (For further information on Hunter, see the following entry.)

Inside, beyond the vestibule, the visitor comes upon a splendid pair of cast aluminium doors of heroic proportions with a design in high relief, which were commissioned for the gallery from Eduardo Paolozzi. The first paintings we come across beyond the doors are from the 17th century. This sets the relationship here between old and new, between the art of the past and the work of our contemporaries.

The rooms are laid out conventionally according to the theories of the 1970s. The ceiling and the battery of rooflights and artifical lights are unattractive, but there is no need to look at them and they serve their function

Stubbs, Moose, painted for Hunter in 1770

well. The main spaces are divided up by the high movable screens that were characteristic of museum design of the period. The wooden floor and the fawn wall coverings may not enliven the appearance of the rooms – this is a function that is left to the pictures themselves.

And the collection is an important one. William Hunter had acquired some truly outstanding works, like the beautiful little Rembrandt sketch of the Entombment (which has survived all the recent purges of Rembrandt's oeuvre) and a fine Dutch 17th century landscape by Koninck. He commissioned Stubbs to paint subjects that interested him in connection with his medical researches and, most surprisingly, he bought three major paintings by the French 18th century artist Chardin while he was still alive, perhaps directly from the painter himself.

The second significant phase of the collection's history was the Birnie Philip Gift (1935) and bequest (1958). Miss Birnie Philip was Whistler's sister-in-law, and her contribution consists for the most part of the contents of Whistler's studio at his death. It includes a series of full-length portraits of women, a big painted screen in two parts, some magical little street scenes, the artist's painting equipment, and groups of silver plate and Oriental blue and white china that were in his house. Knowing Whistler's fastidiousness, and that these things never left his studio, it is not surprising that some of the paintings have the look of being unfinished or rubbed down and put aside. Rather than detracting from the value of the display, it tends to make the artist's presence more immediate, as we might have experienced it on coming into his studio in his lifetime.

Beyond is a fairly strong representation of more recent Scottish and British art, from McTaggart to the 'Scottish Colourists', and then a room devoted to recent British, principally Scottish, work, which is made up of a combination of loans as well as gifts and purchases. There is also a small collection of French 19th century art including Corot, Pissarro and Rodin.

Charles Rennie Mackintosh, guest room furniture, 1919

The Print Gallery houses a very good permanent display illustrating the several processes of print-making, and there is a continuous series of temporary exhibitions drawn from the University's large and important collection of prints, which range from Dürer and Mantegna to some of the younger artists of today.

Outside is a sculpture court, which has somewhat the appearance of an afterthought. It is austere, with a flooring of gravel, stone slabs and brick, and a background for the sculptures of tooled cement, the whole area overshadowed by the library building that towers above it. Yet it must be said that the sculpture on display, which is mostly of metal and all of it recently created, for example works by Anthony Caro and Paolozzi, looks quite at home in this environment.

A special feature of the gallery is the reconstruction of a Victorian terrace house that was substantially rebuilt inside by Charles Rennie Mackintosh and lived in by him and his wife Margaret in the years before the First World War. Windows and doorway are in fact apparent on the outside of the museum building near the main entrance, oddly but not unattractively perched above the level of the pathway. The house is entered through a gallery devoted to contemporary works, some of them recently commissioned by the

University from Scottish artists. The interior decoration of the Mackintosh House gives an extremely good idea of the masterly Mackintosh aesthetic – uniquely consistent and uniquely uncomfortable. You walk into a work of art (with clean shoes please, because the carpet is white). As at the Mackintosh house at Helensburgh, you feel that any personal additions would utterly vitiate the total effect – a perfect museum piece.

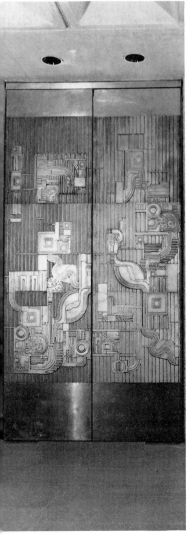

Eduardo Paolozzi doors to Art Gallery

Hunterian Museum

University of Glasgow, Glasgow
G12 8QQ   (041) 330 4221
Closed Sundays. **F** 🖼
♿ to main displays; gallery round main hall, with archaeology and geology displays primarily for students, only accessible by stairs.
♿ & ♿ welcome but must book with Museum Secretary
(041) 339 8855 ext. 4384

William Hunter (1718–83) was renowned as anatomist, physician and medical teacher. He was an intellectual who associated with the circle of Dr Johnson, David Garrick and Horace Walpole. His collecting was no mere fad. It was made partly, but by no means entirely, to further his scientific researches. The extraordinary breadth of his collections is a reflection of his wide-ranging interests. For instance his collection of stones and coral served to further his enquiry into the current belief that all natural phenomena formed an unbroken 'Chain of Being', and that there must therefore be links between living organisms and inert substances, of which coral was thought to be the key.

The Hunterian Museum was opened to the public in Glasgow in 1807, originally in a building like a Greek temple, within the precincts of Glasgow University in the High Street. It was moved with the University to the Hillhead area in 1870, which made it harder for the public to find. However the museum is now well advertised at the main gates and frequent signposts save you from getting lost on the way.

The entrance hall contains an exhibition on the story of the University itself, 'An overflowing fountain'. With a good balance of explanations and real objects to look at, it contrives to give a strong flavour of the struggle, both personal and political, of the scholars of the Middle Ages and Reformation periods, and a sense of the excitement in the discoveries and inventions of the 18th century and later. There are good sections on three of the University's luminaries: William Hunter himself,

'The Overflowing Fountain' exhibition

the engineer James Watt, who began as an instrument maker in the University, and Lord Kelvin, who took his name from the nearby River Kelvin.

Hunter's coin collection contained over 30,000 items. The bulk of them are Greek and Roman, the earliest from the crude coinage current in pre-6th century Greece, but there are medieval Scottish coins as well. The collection has been added to and is now almost twice the size, and one of the most important in Britain. Hunter spent over £20,000 (£1.5 million or more in today's money) on them. When his collections were brought up from London, most of them came by sea, but the coins were sent by road in a wagon 'escorted by six trusty men accustomed to the use of arms.' Yet in the 1850s the coins were described in a University memorandum as a white elephant. Fortunately they survived this contempt and they can now be seen – and enjoyed – in an extremely well thought-out display, which caters at different levels for all stages of knowledge from the complete beginner to the expert numismatist. There are numerous highlights, such as what the thirty pieces of silver were like, or the first Scottish coins to be struck.

Gold 'bonnet piece' coin of James V

Beyond the coin display is a large gallery on the old museum principle with a central rooflight and a balcony running round. The ground floor contains selections from the University's collections of ethnography, Greek and Egyptian antiquities, and fossils, including a dinosaur's footprints and a display on the descent of man. In the centre is a recently arranged display on the Romans in Scotland 80–212 AD, which concentrates particularly on the living conditions of the Roman army at the time. Beyond is an area that is used for temporary exhibitions. The exhibition during autumn 1988 was an excellent one of dugout canoes, skin-boats and elegant sewn-plank boats. Other parts of the hall·were then being re-arranged, and further innovations are planned for the near future.

The balcony upstairs is devoted to geology and Scottish prehistory. The first part is on the now well-known palaeontologist Stan Wood, who worked for a time at the Hunterian, and the remarkable fossils he found in Bearsden, Glasgow, during 1981/2, especially the Bearsden shark, *Stethacanthus nov. sp.* Further on are displays that are intended primarily for university students who are studying the subject, a useful reminder of the primary function of the university museum. Here, too, some of the beautiful polished agates and other stones from Hunter's original collection are included.

Hunter's collection of paintings, itself extremely distinguished, has now been moved to the **Hunterian Art Gallery** over the road.

Museum of Transport

Kelvin Hall, 1 Bunhouse Road,
Glasgow G3 8DP   (041) 357 3929
Open daily. 🇫 ▣ 🅿   ♿W
🏛 contact Friends Society
(GAGMA) for guided tours.
⚥ contact Glasgow Museums
Education Service (041) 334 1131.

The taxi driver expressed his approval of my destination, a rare accolade for any museum. It was moved to its new quarters in the Kelvin Hall building in 1988. The whole atmosphere is new, inviting and exciting, in the spirit of modern museums and in the spirit of Glasgow – it is free and there is something for everybody.

The main hall is a great open space, the roofing left strictly functional and painted out in light grey. There is the confused hubbub of the kind you get in big interior spaces like airports and railway termini, or like the hall of the **Glasgow Art Gallery & Museum** over the road, and this is usually supplemented by piped music. Every light that can be turned on is turned on, so that the visitor is made to feel that he has come to the right place at the right time.

There is an imaginary cobbled Glasgow street of 1938 on a winter afternoon (more lights here, particularly in the shop windows), with vintage cars and delivery tricycles at the kerbside. One of the entrances is to a 'cinema' of the period, usually buzzing with children watching videos (on the occasion of my first visit there was a good interactive video on road safety provided by Glasgow police). Another special area is a reconstruction of the old Glasgow underground railway, and there is a model of the workings of the cable haulage system of 1896.

Among the horse-drawn vehicles are two splendidly painted Romany caravans (their interiors lit up and open to view of course); the old Glasgow-to-London mail coach with a full complement of passengers and baggage (colour plate 7); the two-horse hearse from Ardrishaig; a traction engine from Cambuslang; a threshing machine of 1896 from Sandbach (not all exhibits are from Scotland), and an array of carriages, coaches, gigs, broughams, drays and floats, many of them given or lent to the museum. There are some rare old motors of the first decade of the century and some real aristocrats proudly flaunting their brass head lamps.

View of main hall

Reading caravan built by Duntons, 1918

There are separate displays of fire engines going back to 1900, locomotives, which are kept down to a manageable number for the layman, and a fleet of trams with a high-level walkway running beside them. The railway display includes the royal coach of King George VI, which is on loan from the National Railway Museum at York. A touching relic is the elegant breakfast barrow that was wheeled onto the platform at Aberdeen when the royal train passed on its way to Balmoral.

Cars from the 1930s onwards are wittily displayed in a 'motor showroom', with their details, including their price when they were new, displayed on the windscreen. Elsewhere the labels are clear, brief, legible and unobtrusive.

Upstairs is a more conventional array of historic bicycles and motorcycles, enlivened by early prams, a drunks' barrow and the Sinclair C5. Beside it is the 'Clyde Room'. This is a very large area with an extremely impressive array of ships' models, which have been collected by the museum for a long time, set out in roughly chronological order. The models are mainly of ships built on the Clyde for different destinations worldwide, up to the model of an oil rig of 1966. The display is essential for anyone with a special knowledge or interest in ship design, although its sheer extent is rather daunting to the ordinary visitor.

A well illustrated guide to the museum is designed to act as a souvenir as well, and there is a separate guide to the ship model collection.

People's Palace Museum

Glasgow Green, Glasgow G40 1AT
(041) 554 0223
Open daily. 🄵 🄼 🄿
&: wheelchair access via winter gardens to ground floor; lift and **T** should be installed by end of 1990.
🏛 contact Museum Secretary.
👫 contact Glasgow Museums Education Service (041) 334 1131.

If you want to know about Glasgow, one of the places you have to visit is the People's Palace. Sited appropriately on the edge of Glasgow Green, on the far side from the Gorbals Cross, it was conceived in 1866 but was not actually opened until 1898, when Lord Rosebery described its purpose rather curiously as 'a palace of pleasure and imagination around which the people may place their affections and which may give them a home on which their memory may rest.' Now, 90 years on, after a period of serious decline following the last war, it is being visited by around 400,000 people a year, most of them people who live nearby and who treat it as their neighbourhood museum, much as Lord Rosebery had hoped.

This is not surprising. The building includes a magnificent glass winter garden, where the museum has a café. The museum itself is devoted exclusively to the history of Glasgow. It has

The winter garden

been said that the history we learn there is too much slanted to the working classes and their struggle, for example through the period of the First World War and the development of the unions. Yet for anyone coming on the city from the outside, it is hard to see how the story of its people could be written otherwise, especially on the edge of Glasgow Green, where so much of the early history of the trade union movement in Britain was acted out.

If you prefer your history to leave out the embarrassment of some of these times, it is perhaps better not to come. If you want to know about it, and if you want to catch something of the warmth of spirit that has surrounded the place and the people, you will find it still clinging to the People's Palace. I don't know any other museum with a resident cat, and Smudge is naturally a favourite of the younger habitués.

The most interesting part of the earlier section tells of the origins of Glasgow's prosperity, which was based on the tobacco trade. The 19th century themes treated on the first floor tend to run rapidly into one another: the suffragettes; the Great War and the industrial strife after it; a model lodging house; the movies of the 1920s; Private Towser, the nigger minstrel's dog; the temperance movement; the age of rock; and on the stair to the next landing a portrait of Billy Connolly by John Byrne.

These things are punctuated by a number of reconstructed scenes: a printer's workshop of 1783; a chemist's shop; a dairy; a general store; a splendid Victorian bathroom made up of individual pieces that have been brought together. Particular items catch the eye, like the painting of a shopkeeper of the 1790s (ill. on cover); or the stained-glass image of a glass blower of 1878; or a bobbin stand made by a brass finisher in his spare time, and a model blacksmith with his forge, both made in 1883.

A separate room is devoted to a changing display drawn from the museum's collection of stained glass that was being made in Glasgow in a number of very distinguished studios

One of Ken Currie's eight scenes of Glasgow's industrial history, 1986–87

Painting by an unknown artist of a Glasgow shopkeeper, 1790s

during the 19th century. It is called the Cottier Room, after the principal producer.

Glasgow Museums recently commissioned one of the younger generation of Glasgow painters, Ken Currie, to paint for the People's Palace eight episodes in Glasgow's industrial history beginning with the Calton weavers' strike of 1787. These go right round underneath the huge cupola on the first floor, in dark red, orange and black with occasional flashes of strong blue.

What we can learn from the permanent collection is supplemented partly by a series of temporary exhibitions on subjects related to the city, and partly by a series of studies written on different aspects of Glasgow life: for example 'Glasgow Green', 'Scotland Sober and Free' on the temperance movement, an account of the stained glass industry, 'The Strike of the Glasgow Weavers 1787', and a full history and guide to the Palace itself. These make fascinating reading, though it has to be said that the quality of their printing has not always matched the high standard of the research that has gone into their writing. The temporary exhibitions are characterised, like the publications, by an instinct for interesting subjects. The displays themselves however are not backed by any very sophisticated visual sense, and they are produced on too small a budget. Indeed, although the People's Palace is a member of the group of museums maintained by the City Council, the visitor will find none of the polish and impression of prosperity that he finds in the new **Museum of Transport** or the **Burrell Collection**. There are hopeful indications that the situation may be improved in the near future.

What comes through, in permanent displays and temporary exhibitions alike, is an infectious enthusiasm for the chosen themes and the people who are their subject. The very profusion of evidence, although much of it trivial in itself – caricatures, posters and the like – has a way of adding up to an impression of what it was like at the time.

[A new medieval gallery opened in autumn 1989. Ed.]

GOLSPIE (H)

Dunrobin Castle Museum

Dunrobin, Golspie KW10 62A
(04083) 3177
Closed October to May. ♿ to Dunrobin Castle. ▣ ℗
♿: inaccessible to the disabled.
♿ & ♿ contact Administrator or Curator.

This museum, which is in the grounds at Dunrobin at a little distance from the house, is fascinating just as much for the ordinary visitor as for the connoisseur of museums, and it is as yet far too little known. Whilst historic houses in private hands, like the properties belonging to the National Trust for Scotland, have mostly been excluded from this guide, there was no question that this was a case for making an exception.

The building that houses the museum was originally an elegant summerhouse, built in 1732, approached by a steep flight of stone steps. In 1878 it was turned into a museum and an

One of the ethnographical showcases

Pictish cross slab found at Golspie

extension was built on behind, so that the entrance from the original summerhouse now brings you into the extension at first floor level. The extension's interior is made entirely of wood with a skylight running down the middle of the roof. A gallery goes down the two long sides and curves round at the end.

The first impression is of stepping into a museum that has not been changed since it was made over a century ago. To some extent this is true, and the family intend to keep it that way. One reason for this impression is that the objects are arranged decoratively, everything being made to follow as far as possible a symmetrical design. The display in the extension is dominated by a series of antlers hung from the cross beams and round the outside of the gallery, with a ship's figurehead at the centre of the rounded gallery.

The main feature of the summerhouse, which also has a balcony round three sides, is a collection of animal heads (there are said to be around 250 altogether). There are also stuffed

Interior of the original building looking through to the museum extension of 1878

Sutherland (1888–1963) and his wife Eileen, on sporting expeditions throughout the world, expertly stuffed by the taxidermist Rowland Ward (so well known that he is immortalised in one of Saki's stories) and now carefully labelled.

In the showcases upstairs in the summerhouse is a considerable ethnographical collection, again put together by members of the family on their expeditions abroad. There are Indian weapons, objects from West Africa, three Javanese shadow puppets, African archery, Indian brasswork and jewellery, marvellous gold-spangled elephant decorations, ivory carvings from the Far East, African beadwork, Inuit (Eskimo) snowshoes, and objects from the Pacific and from North American Indians.

Downstairs in the extension building is an outstanding collection of Pictish stones carved with ornaments and symbols, all of them found at Dunrobin or nearby. Especially notable is a large cross-slab that was used as a gravestone in the churchyard of St Andrew's Church, Golspie.

Along the gallery are mementoes of the Sutherland family, and local geology, fossils and archaeology. A number of finds from over a century ago include silvered-bronze penannular brooches found in 1868 when the railway was being built at Pitfour, Rogart (others are in the Ashmolean Museum, Oxford, and in the **National Museum** in Edinburgh); a number of medieval bronze brooches; two Viking tortoise-shaped brooches found in a long grave near Dunrobin some time before 1885; and a jet necklace from a cairn at Torrish.

The museum has recently been overhauled. The process of cataloguing the collection is in hand – some objects have so far defied identification – and their environmental conditions are being brought up to date. It is sad that in order to finance this operation one of the archaeological treasures of the museum, the Achavrail armlet, had to be sold, although it is some consolation that it went no further than **Inverness**, where it is now one of the prides of the Museum (see p. 62).

animals, birds and reptiles here and in the extension. There is a Whale-headed Stork, a Grant's Gazelle head, a Marine Iguana from the Galapagos, a Buffalo head, and an Oryx head. The head and neck of a Giraffe stand centrally with the tusks of an African Elephant guarding it on either side. Nearby, also symmetrically placed, are two crocodiles stuffed to stand on their hind legs, with jaws open and forefeet joined as if they were used to hold something – perhaps the umbrellas of visitors to the museum.

This grotesque Victorian fancy is in sharp contrast with the high standard of scientific accuracy in the mounting of the animal heads. These are from animals that were shot by members of the family, principally the 5th Duke of

GREENOCK (S)

McLean Museum & Art Gallery

15 Kelly Street, Greenock PA16 8JX
(0475) 23741
Closed until spring 1990.
Thereafter closed Sundays. ▣
♿: wheelchair access to ground
floor only.
🚻 & 🚹 welcome but should book
in advance.

James McLean was a Greenock timber
merchant who provided the endowment for a museum, which was built in
1876. It was joined onto the library of
1835, and built in the same quasi-
ecclesiastical style with gothic finials
and battlements. Inside, the main gallery is a large and impressive hall of the
familiar museum pattern, originally
with rooflights along its length and a
gallery running round at first floor level
supported by iron pillars. The ironwork of the roof trusses, the balustrade
and other decorative details have a
severe elegance.

The building was sadly in need of
repair when the museum was taken
over by Inverclyde District Council in
1975. A major reconstruction programme meant that the collections were
almost entirely taken off display during
1988. It is anticipated that the museum
will be re-opened, with completely reorganised displays, in the spring of
1990. In the reconstructed hall the
rooflights will be covered over in the
interests of conservation. A platform
will be introduced at mezzanine level
over about a third of the floor area, to
accommodate some of the shipping
exhibits.

The ground floor will be set aside
for items of local interest. Pre-eminent
among local industries is shipbuilding, and there is a good collection
of ships' models and maritime machinery. The emphasis is on steam rather
than sail. Among the exhibits is a highly finished model of a turbo engine
from the shipyard of J.G. Kincaid &

David S. Ewart, The Emigrants, *1926*

Co of Greenock, which was made by
apprentices in the first six months of
their training. Complementing this is
the Paterson collection of photographs
of steamers, to which the interested
visitor has ready access.

There will also be displays on the
Gourock ropeworks; on Henry Bell
and the first commercial steamship on
the Clyde, the 'Comet'; on the builder
of the tea clippers, Robert Steele; and
of course Greenock's most famous son,
the engineer James Watt (1736–1819),
who gave his name to the original
library and lecture hall.

The intention to found a museum
goes back to 1861, the date of the
formation of the Greenock Philosophical Society, of which James
McLean was a member. The main
purpose was to build up 'a collection to
illustrate the industries, the Natural
History, and the Antiquities of the
town and its neighbourhood'. Soon
after it was opened, it received a case of
specimens from the Clyde Pottery
Company. The company had already
been going since 1816, and continued
in business until 1905. The specimens

in the gift included not only examples
of the finished wares, but also raw
materials and moulds showing the various stages of manufacture.

Greenock is one of the museums
which, being in a seaport, benefitted

Jug made at the Clyde Pottery

19th century Chinese ivory ship model

HAWICK (B)

Hawick Museum & The Scott Gallery

Wilton Lodge Park, Hawick
Roxburghshire TD9 7JL
(0450) 73457
Closed Sunday mornings, and all
day Saturday October to March.
🍴 but 🄵 to local residents. 🄿
♿ S: first floor and art gallery
inaccessible to wheelchairs.

from gifts of things brought back by sea
captains from their travels. It therefore
has an important ethnographic collection, which is particularly strong in
objects from Japan and the Far East.
The outstanding gift came from David
Swan, Captain of S.S. 'Gulf of Genoa',
whose voyages took him to the South
Pacific, the Red Sea, America, India
and the Far East in the 1890s. Among
his very varied collection is an important group of ritual objects from New
Ireland. A more unusual gift of this
kind is a collection of stuffed animals
and birds. Instead of local wildlife of
the kind we usually meet in our
museums, Greenock has big game, the
gift of local shipbuilder R.L. Scott,
including a sloth bear, a tiger and a
Nile crocodile. In the reconstructed
museum these are ranged along one
side of the balcony, while the ethnographic collections occupy the other
side.

The museum also has an art gallery
element. The nucleus of the permanent collection of paintings came from
a Greenock shipbuilder, Stuart Anderson Caird, who bequeathed his pictures to the museum in 1917, together
with a sum of £6,000 for adding to
them. The main weight of the collection, which Caird intended to be for
the promotion of art in his native town,
is Scottish painting from the mid-19th
century, including paintings of the
Glasgow School and the 'Scottish Colourists', and topographical views of
Greenock and its neighbourhood.

Wilton Lodge was a private house,
built in 1859, standing in fairly extensive grounds. In 1906 house and
grounds were left to Roxburgh District
Council, who made the grounds into a
park for the public and converted the
house into the district museum. The
idea of forming a collection in Hawick,
however, is as old as Wilton Lodge
itself. The Hawick Archaeological
Society was founded in 1856, and the
first of its 'Transactions' were published seven years later. It is the antiquities and other things collected by
the Society that form the core of the
museum's present collections.

Hawick had by then been a long-
standing centre for the knitwear industry, which grew from 18th century
cottage-based workshops into the
hosiery mills on which Hawick's
prosperity was based. There were two
keys to its development. The first was
the use of woollen rather than linen
thread, and the second was the invention of a machine that could knit round
in a circle. These two things combined
to make it possible to produce seamless
stockings, and later other garments,
which would cling neatly to the essentially tubular shape of the human body.

The stages of this development are
well described in a display that has
recently been renewed, tracing the industry from its beginnings with the
activity of Baillie John Hardie (born in
1722), a merchant and magistrate of
Hawick who started a hosiery business
with stocking machines. There are examples of the earliest knitting

machines, like the primitive wooden
construction that was made in Glasgow
and used in Hawick from 1798, as well
as a modern machine made in the
1950s especially for Hawick Museum
by William Cotton Ltd of Lough-
borough.

The people of Hawick have always
retained a fierce spirit of independence, and the framework knitters, or
'frameworkers' as they were called,
were involved with the early history of
trade unions and strikes. Their trade

Model guillotine made by a prisoner of war

Stocking machine used at Hawick from 1798

banner hangs in the hall of the museum.

People will vary in their preference for learning about the industry of Hawick or for browsing among the objects that belong to the original collection – and to an earlier concept of museums. These things, shown mainly in one of the front rooms, include a collection of early spectacles, and boxes for snuff and patches. Antiquities include a fine bronze ewer and cast bronze pot from the 15th century. There is an intriguing fanciful guillotine made of bone, with bone soldiers standing guard round its base, by a Napoleonic prisoner of war in Hawick. There is also an extraordinary three-dimensional working caricature, constructed clumsily out of wood, which shows an enlightened House of Commons with Gladstone and Bright in the teeth of the Obstruction and Retrogression of the House of Lords at the time of the Reform Bill.

The Hawick Room contains a model of the town and district based on a map

of 1824. Hawick is one of the Border towns that keep up the old tradition of the common riding (see **Halliwell's House, Selkirk**). A painting of the Hawick version of the ceremony, made in 1892, gives a very sedate impression. On display are a drum, banner and sword, and other souvenirs of the common riding, including the dress of the cornet.

Wilton Lodge was built with a large open hall and a square gallery above. The entrance area usually houses small temporary exhibits of topical interest. The balcony is used for the display of an unusually attractive group of topographical paintings of Hawick and the surrounding countryside (see ill. on cover), a number of them distinctly 'primitive' in character, and others by local artists who achieved wider fame in Scotland, notably Tom Scott (1854–1927), who is well represented. Also upstairs is a natural history section, including cases of seabirds, moorland birds and owls.

In 1975 the Scott Gallery, a large top-lit gallery, was added to the building. This is used in part to house more of the permanent collection of pictures, and in part to show temporary exhibitions.

3D wooden Reform Bill 'caricature'

INVERNESS (H)

Inverness Museum & Art Gallery

Castle Wynd, Inverness IV2 3ED
(0463) 237114
Closed Sundays, except during July and August. **F ▣**
&. A: ground floor (including cafeteria) accessible to wheelchairs; stairs to first floor.

The first exhibit you meet, at the entrance to the main hall, is a beautiful osprey in flight. This introduces one of the three principal displays, on the natural history of the Highlands; the other two are on prehistoric and medieval life there, and – a factor that plays an important part by virtue of Highland geography – transport and communication.

Osprey in flight

The Achavrail armlet

Reconstruction of taxidermist's shop

The museum's present building, on the site of the original 19th century one, dates from 1966. The origin of the collection, however, goes back to the founding of the Northern Institution for the Promotion of Science and Literature in 1825. The hall is large and open, mostly artifically lit, with black wood-effect ceiling and supporting pillars and the various sections in separate bays. It is an attractive arrangement that leaves an impression of spaciousness. To one side is the museum shop with a good selection of literature on life in the Highlands.

The cases showing the different aspects of Highland wildlife are lively and informative, with displays centring for example on a golden eagle or a red deer calf. A particular distinction of the museum is a care for language, which leads to bilingual labels in English and Gaelic, and extends to some attention – almost unique in museums in Britain – to the needs of French and German tourists who do not read English. Near to the natural history displays are notes about the Highland Biological Recording Group with an invitation for people to take part in research on the countryside.

The archaeology section begins with the view out of the window towards Craig Phadrig, a hill fort built around 400–200 BC. Reconstructions of life in early and medieval times are not very convincing, but this is made up for by an extremely helpful and sensible emphasis on the sites themselves, with

photographs and notes on visiting them, for example 'Private land – please ask at the farm'. A recent acquisition is the Achavrail armlet from **Dunrobin Museum**. It will no doubt take its place here soon beside the replicas of gold armlets and the photograph of three Pictish brooches from near Croy, all of which are in Edinburgh.

Particularly good is the section on communications, which brings home vividly the extent to which any kind of material progress in this mostly hostile terrain relies upon transport. The account begins with the old drove roads for bringing cattle across the hills to market, and then the 243 miles of military roadway built by General Wade in the 1730s as a necessary step towards controlling the rebellious Highlanders. After this the display takes us through civilian and commercial developments, starting with Thomas Telford in the late 18th century: the stage coach from 1811; the Caledonian Canal, which let ships through from east to west; then the Highland railway, which opened up the way south as much as bringing people north. The account comes up to date with the Kessock Bridge of 1892 and a section on air travel.

The art gallery element is not a main attraction for the visitor from outside the Highlands. The permanent collection is mainly Scottish, with a local emphasis. A gallery is reserved for temporary exhibitions, mostly brought in from elsewhere.

Travelling Punch and Judy show

The main displays upstairs are on local history, and especially the crafts practised in the Highlands. There are some splendid individual pieces, like the Murdoch pistols, and a good section on the making of the bagpipe. The last taxidermist's shop to survive in Inverness, reconstituted in the gallery, represents what was a flourishing Victorian trade supported by highland shooting parties. Even as late as 1935, we learn, 162 stags' heads were mounted in this shop during the months of September and October.

A reconstructed silversmith's shop leads to a display of distinguished and often extremely elegant silverware. It ranges from communion cups to spoons and toddy ladles, and 'quaichs' – the bowls in which whisky was passed from mouth to mouth on festive occasions. The heyday of Inverness silver was in the early 19th century, but the earliest pieces go back to the 1730s.

The museum was at one time known particularly for its Jacobite relics. In fact it was described in 1908 as being mainly 'a Highland and Jacobite collection'. The history of the Jacobites is a vital and vivid chapter of the Highland story, and the fact that so much legend grew up round it is a reflection of its importance and of the nature of life in the Highlands. But scholars do not live happily with legends, and this side of the collection is now reduced to a single case of memorabilia, most of them described with due caution as 'said to be' connected with Bonnie Prince Charlie.

IRVINE (S)

Scottish Maritime Museum

*Laird Forge, Gottries Road, Irvine
KA12 8QE   (0294) 78283*
Closed November to March. 🆂 🅿
♿ **S**: the ships inaccessible to
wheelchairs and difficult for the
disabled.
🚼 & 🍴 welcome.

The remit of the museum, as its name
implies, covers the maritime history of
Scotland. What is to be seen at any one
time is not a permanent display, and
the intention is that it should be treated
as a working museum. Visitors can see
boat-builders, riggers, painters and fit-
ters at work on restoration and reproduction projects. They can go on board
some of the ships, and are encouraged
to talk to the museum's research workers, who may be able to track down
information on boats and the men who
sailed in them.

The museum is based at Irvine's
large former shipyard. It is a complex
consisting at present of three compo-
nents, two of them on the harbourside.
The boat shop, a large newly-built
hangar, houses a different display each
year. In 1988 various types of boat
construction were shown. These were
typified by very specific boats, and their
histories were given on display boards.
For example there was the Loch
Broom Post Boat, in use up to the
1920s but now far from seaworthy,
whose character is of the 18th century;
there was the extremely elegant shape
of the four-oar racer, 'Mary Chalmers'; and dominating the space was
the great hull of the schooner, 'Lady
Guilford', built at Rothesay for the
Marquess of Bute in 1819. There were
fishing boats, too, but the museum
acknowledges the high reputation and
competence of the **Scottish Fisheries
Museum** at **Anstruther**, and does not
seek to compete with it.

150 yards down the quayside are the
Pontoons, at which a changing array of
craft is moored. Apart from some elegant small sailing yachts, the visitor is
left free to walk over whatever boats are

Inside the boat shop

open for inspection. In the summer of
1988 there were three of these: the
1950 lifeboat, 'St Cybi', on permanent
loan from the RNLI; the 1956 tug,
'Garnock', that used to work in Irvine
harbour, presented in 1984; and 'Spartan', the last of the surviving 'puffers'
from Kirkintilloch. 'Spartan' was built
in 1942 for the Royal Navy, for taking
supplies to the fleet, and was afterwards turned to carrying bricks and
coal between Troon and Rothesay.
Under restoration was 'TGB', the
Longhope lifeboat, which was salvaged
after it was tragically overwhelmed by
the sea with her crew of eight in 1969.
[The Longhope lifeboat will be the
principal feature of the museum's displays in 1990, 'The Cruel Sea', on the
theme of rescue and disaster. Ed.]

It will not seem particularly strange
that vessels like the Post Boat from
Loch Broom or Lord Bute's schooner
should be described affectionately, as
they are, but surprising to the layman
that some of the iron monsters at the
museum are treated in the same spirit.
The fact is that each vessel, although it
may have been recruited as an example
of its class, is regarded as an individual

The 'Lady Guilford' being moved into the boat shop

Workshop at Laird Forge

with a personality and a history of its own, and this sense of caring is easily transmitted to the visitor.

Not far from the quayside is the Tenement Building, where the visitor can see a reconstruction of a shipyard worker's flat of 1910. This seems to suggest that the conditions in which the workers were living at this time, in the heyday of the Scottish shipyards, although certainly cramped, were hardly more so than that of workers in other industries in Scotland and were otherwise reasonably prosperous.

The visitor is well supplied with notes (provided in the form of handy leaflets) on what is to be seen at the moment, and on future projects. The museum is only five years old, and showing every sign of rapid and ambitious development.

The most ambitious of the plans for the future was already half way through in the summer of 1988. This is the removal (which has already been carried out) and the subsequent re-erection of the engine shop from Stephen's of Linthouse at Govan. This giant hangar, 200 ft long, 'a veritable cathedral of cast-iron, timber and glass' was built in 1872. It will be used to house the collection of industrial machinery, some of which it is planned to have in working order.

KILMARNOCK (S)

Dean Castle

Dean Road, Kilmarnock KA3 1XB
(0563) 22702/26401 ext. 36
Open daily. 🈺 but 🅵 to children and residents. 🖵 🅿
♿ S: steep stairs to upper floors.
🚹 & 🚺 welcome but must book in advance.

The castle belonged originally to the Boyd family, the Lords of Kilmarnock. The keep is thought to date from the mid-14th century; the palace and 'barmkin', or outer wall, were added about a hundred years later. Around 1908 Thomas Evelyn Ellis, 8th Lord Howard de Walden, acquired the castle and restored it over the next 30 years. He put back the oldest part, the keep, to something like its original condition. The palace banqueting hall was embellished with panels and a 17th century plaster ceiling which were brought from another building. A gatehouse was added, and so was a covered gallery over the outer wall. Apart from the interest of the building itself, the castle qualifies as a museum mainly by virtue of two collections, both of which are exhibited in the keep.

Lord Howard's father-in-law Charles Van Raalte collected early musical instruments. These are mostly stringed instruments such as violins, lutes and harps, but there are also a number of small keyboard instruments (colour plate 1), some of them extremely unusual. It seems clear that Van Raalte's enthusiasm was for the beautiful craftsmanship of the instruments, rather than the history of their development or a love of the sound they made. Looking at some of the pieces he was able to collect, this is thoroughly understandable. They are fastidiously displayed, if we forgive the obtrusiveness of some of the labels, and placed whenever appropriate on a mirror so that the workmanship of their backs can be appreciated. Several instruments are of great historical significance, representing the work of

famous instrument makers of the 16th, 17th and 18th centuries.

Lord Howard himself, inspired perhaps by his father-in-law or by a sense of appropriateness to the castle, made a collection of armour and weapons. The collection is not extensive, but it is extremely select. As with the musical instruments, the impression is given of someone collecting from an admiration for craftsmanship rather than from a devotion to military his-

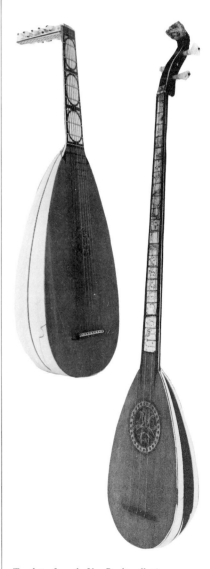

Two lutes from the Van Raalte collection

French parade helmet, c.1560

KINGUSSIE (H)

Highland Folk Museum

Duke Street, Kingussie PH21 1JG
(05402) 307
Closed Saturdays and Sundays
November to March. 🔊 🅿
♿ **W**: all main routes to exhibition
buildings suitable for wheelchairs.
🚻 & 🚻 contact Admin. Assistant.

It all began with Dr Isobel Grant. Inspired by a new type of museum devoted to folk life which she saw in Scandinavia, she set up a folk museum in an old church on Iona in the 1930s to preserve a record of the Highland way of life that was fast disappearing. It was the first folk museum in Britain. It was later moved to the centre of Kingussie, sited incongruously enough between a graveyard and a railway line, to form the basis of the present museum.

Three different buildings of traditional Highland types have been reconstructed here (or built up from new). One is a blackhouse from the Isle of Lewis, with the cow byre inside the door and an earth floor throughout. Some of the smoke from the central hearth, when it is lit, finds its way up through the turf in the ceiling, providing potash for the ground for the next season. In the summer the visitor may be greeted by a Highland woman offering the oatcakes or scones she is making. Nearby is a 'clack mill' of the kind used in the Isle of Lewis, and further on a large 'turf house'. As protection from the elements is provided by growing turf with its moss and weeds all over the roof and walls, this looks strangely like a house-shaped hillock. It was built experimentally on the cruck principle a few years ago, and its weaknesses in standing up to winter weather have proved helpful in revealing how these houses were actually built.

A large modern hangar, the Farming Museum, is not the usual collection of farming implements laid out in rows but a much livelier – if more selective – presentation for the ordinary townsman to see. Dominating the first area is

tory. The armour is mainly of German or Italian workmanship, and includes three parade helmets of exceptional elegance and sophistication; there is also an impressive group of swords.

A curious full-length portrait of the Baron, which hangs with the armour in the great hall of the keep, shows him in Spanish costume a few years before he acquired the castle, and is painted in the style of Velasquez which was popular at that time. In fact we get a good deal closer to the man's character in a bronze bust made of him by Rodin, which is shown in the banqueting hall of the palace. Lord Howard did not have many years to enjoy his finished residence, for he died in 1946. The castle and the surrounding park were

given to the town of Kilmarnock by his son in 1975, and it is now administered by Kilmarnock and Loudoun District Museums.

Normally part of the castle is available by open access – this includes an important part of the musical instrument collection in the banqueting hall. The rest of the castle can be seen only by guided tour, which is no doubt necessary for reasons of security. Museum goers may regret this restriction. In practice however the tour usually lasts for about an hour, and there is ample time for most people to enjoy the collections. People with a specialised interest in either collection may do well to make special arrangements in advance.

Kitchen tableau in the Macrobert House

KIRKCALDY (F)

Kirkcaldy Museum & Art Gallery

War Memorial Gardens, Kirkcaldy, Fife KY1 1YG   (0592) 260732
Open daily. **F** ▣ opening spring 1990.
♿: first floor inaccessible to wheelchairs.
🏛 & ♟ welcome; phone in advance for special facilities (handling sessions etc.). ◉

The principal exhibition area on the ground floor is a general introduction to the district and its main characteristics: 'Changing Places: river, coal and sea'. The space is so partitioned that we are led on a winding route past a continuous arrangement of showcases, so that we come across a succession of tall, very narrow display panels. Objects are often quite low down in the cases, and every opportunity is taken to leave things outside the glass of the case with a direct invitation to touch – two indications that the interests of young visitors are kept firmly in mind. The narrow panels mean that single features of the district or its history are presented one at a time. A virtue of the display is that different themes, different places and different periods are interwoven, without being forced into a chronological or geographical strait-jacket.

The first objects in their narrow enclosure come as something of a shock: an Edwardian table and chairs elaborately carved out of parrot coal and highly polished. The archaeology of the Wemyss Caves, a display of axe-heads, prehistoric food vessels and an early bronze dagger, or the coins associated with Mary Queen of Scots, may come next door to a panel showing the wildlife in the modern town, and near to a description of Glenrothes new town, or a lighthearted reminder of Kirkcaldy as a seaside resort. It is an effective introduction to the distinctive features of the area – and a museum

a scene with a tinker at work and the things he made (baskets, brooms, horn spoons and silver brooches as well as saucepans). There are photographs and a description of the role of the travelling people in the life of the Highlands, which was more important than is generally appreciated.

The distinguishing characteristic of this museum is that it is (unusually) a Regional rather than a District Museum. It is therefore concerned not with a limited area but with life in the whole of the Highlands and Islands. So there are opportunities here to compare differences in local practice, just as the reconstruction of Highland buildings has been used as an opportunity to discover how these buildings were made. The displays give evidence not only of the research that lies behind them, which is still being actively pursued, but of an unsentimental affection for the traditions of the crofting communities and the practical good sense that lay behind them in areas where resources were scarce.

Further on in the Farming Museum are a woman dragging a harrow from North Uist, and a sledge for moving stones over rough ground called a 'puddock' (made of heavy forked branches, it is indeed roughly frog-like).

Flails are shown with photographs and notes on men using them, and close to the threshing machines that were to replace them. Harness includes pack saddles and a horse collar made of woven grass from North Uist. The display ends with notes on the last stage coach in Britain, which plied between Kingussie and Laggan up to 1914, and a splendid fire engine with a steam pump from Ballindalloch Estate.

In another building is an excellent collection of furniture from Argyll, Orkney, Skye, Wester Ross, Harris and elsewhere. The way the chairs were made in places where wood was scarce is particularly fascinating. There is a box bed from Badenoch, dated 1702, and a beautiful copper travelling trunk studded with brass nails from Inverness. And there are spinning wheels of different kinds, and notes on spinning and weaving. In the main building are displays of old tartans and the dyes used for them; fiddles, bagpipes and clarsachs (the Scottish harps); and kitchen and cooking equipment (much of it made by the local blacksmith – or indeed by the tinker).

The shop is well provided with literature on the Highlands, including an account of the building of the turf house.

Group of Wemyss ware

early work, and the unusually gentle near-abstraction of 'The Wave'.

The second determining factor is support from Shell Oil, whose interest in Moss Moran has led to their concern for community involvement. This support is being invested shrewdly in contemporary Scottish art, and one of the rooms of the gallery is reserved for this, and includes at the same time regularly changing displays of craftwork.

Downstairs there is also a permanent display of the older kinds of pottery made locally. The highlight is Wemyss Ware, whose exuberant designs were at their best in the early part of the 20th century. (A new display of Wemyss Ware will be incorporated in the Wemyss Café, opening here in spring 1990.) Four rooms are reserved for temporary exhibitions, which range from travelling exhibitions originating elsewhere in Scotland to the annual Fife art exhibition in November.

display of this kind, however detailed or insistent, can hardly achieve more than that.

We are introduced to the coal mines; to fishing and whaling (900 tons of whale oil were landed in Kirkcaldy in 1833); to the shipyards of Kinghorn and Burntisland; to the Kirkcaldy potteries. The growth of the linoleum industry, for which Kirkcaldy became famous, is fully described (flax for its manufacture was readily available as the linen industry was well established here when Sir Michael Barker Nairn took on the recent linoleum patent in 1887). We also meet the great men of Kirkcaldy, like two of the greatest architects of the Georgian period in Britain, William Adam and his son Robert; Adam Smith, who wrote *The Wealth of Nations* (1776) in Kirkcaldy; and more recently John Thompson, the Celtic goalie.

The museum was built as part of the War Memorial Gardens in 1925, with money provided by John Nairn, the

owner of the principal Kirkcaldy linoleum factory. Rather unusually, the library was added as an afterthought rather than the other way round.

The collection of paintings on the first floor is by no means a poor relation. It has two principal elements. The first of these, both in date and in size, is due to Mr Blyth, a Kirkcaldy linen manufacturer who had a strong taste for art. Blyth was a leading light in the museum's council and his personal collection was acquired when he died in 1964. It gives the museum's collection a character that it might otherwise lack. Mr Blyth's particular interests were the work of William McTaggart (1835–1910), and paintings from the early 20th century by the 'Scottish colourists' – S.J. Peploe, F.C.B. Cadell and Leslie Hunter – and by Walter Sickert and the Camden Town Group. Particularly noteworthy are a group of paintings by Peploe and another by McTaggart, which includes characteristic landscapes as well as some of his

'Beside the Seaside' display

KIRKCUDBRIGHT
(D)

The Stewartry Museum

*St Mary Street, Kirkcudbright
DG6 4AQ   (0557) 31643*
Closed November to Easter,
otherwise closed Sundays. ◩
&: first floor inaccessible to
disabled.
⛶ & ⛶ welcome but must book in
advance.

The museum was first opened in 1881
in the Town Hall, but within a few
years the present building was erected
to house the growing collections, financed entirely by public subscription.
Opened in 1892, it is in dark grey and
red sandstone, decorated with somewhat unusual castellations, turrets and
thistle finials. The interior is mainly a
large open hall, with a narrow balcony
supported by tall iron pillars running
round the sides (elegance is not its
strong point).

The exhibits are displayed in showcases round the walls and in the centre
of the main hall, grouped according to
the nature of the objects and their use,
and identified with simple handwritten
descriptions. There is an engaging
profusion of ear trumpets, spinning
wheels, clay pipes, early spectacles and

sewing machines, witches' stones,
snuff boxes and communion tokens.
More specifically local in character are
the geological samples of local stone,
and axe-heads and fossils found in the
area.

A characteristic of the museum is a
strong romantic streak, which finds an
echo in many of us, though it may
sometimes conflict with historical
truth. There is the horn cup made by
Billy Marshall, a colourful local character described as the King of the
Galloway Tinker Gypsies (the local
word is 'tinkler'), who died in 1792
reputedly at the age of 120 years; the
engine of the first motor car in the
district of Stewartry before the reg-
istration of motor vehicles was introduced; and a bottle that was found
filled with brandy in 1820 in a smug-
gler's hiding place at Nunton Farm,
Twynholm, and was used as a whisky
bottle by a man in Millhall up to about
1890.

A flintlock blunderbuss, with 'London' and 'GENL POST OFFICE'
engraved on the butt plate, was carried
on the Stranraer mail coach in the late
18th century. Then there is a case of
works by Joseph Heugham, a Victorian
blacksmith of Auchencairn, a few miles
to the east of Kirkcudbright, who had a
reputation as a scholar and poet.

A curious small round box served as
a Jacobite and Catholic reliquary. The
box is Italian, enamelled with the Stewart tartan, and has a false lid bearing a

Medieval bronze tripod ewer and pot

portrait of the Bonnie Prince on it. The
inside has a sparkling ground, strangely
crenellated sides with little reels, and
five minarets, a complex gold one at
the centre, with four labels: *Corporalis*,
Holy Cross, S. Macelli M, and *Agnus
Dei*. It is said to have been given by
Bonnie Prince Charlie to Clementina
Walkinshaw after she had looked after
him in a cottage at Culloden during the
1745 rebellion.

The town clock of Kirkcudbright,
dating from about 1600, is here, and an
old photograph shows it in its original
position. It is distinguished for having
only an hour hand, and no minute
hand. Five iron candlesticks, called
'carles', come from different places in
the locality. There is a witness box on
castors, which was in use from 1868 to
1971 in Kirkcudbright Court House,
and – if the identification is correct – a
mesolithic barbed spear point made
from the antler of a red deer, brought
up from the bed of the River Dee in
1895.

A small side room is devoted to local
shipping, partly celebrating John Paul
Jones, who was born in 1747 in Kirk-
bean, Kirkcudbrightshire, served part
of his early training as a seaman at
Kirkcudbright, and became commander of the American navy and its first
great hero.

Artists connected with Kirkcudbright are represented, notably the
illustrator Jessie M. King (1875–
1949). But the most distinguished
artist is E.A. Hornel (1864–1933), who
is worthily and fascinatingly evoked by

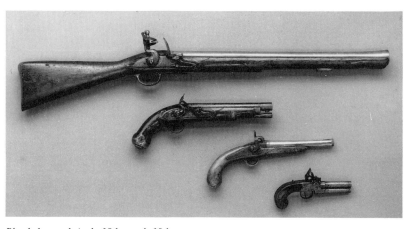

Blunderbuss and pistols, 18th to early 19th century

is studio and Japanese garden in *Broughton House* down the road.

The balcony is used to show the fish and birds that are to be found in the Stewartry. We do not know how much there may have been originally in the way of wonders from overseas. The founder and honorary curator of the museum for 25 years was a naval man, John McKie RN, which suggests that part of the original motive for the museum may have been to show to the people of Kirkcudbright those 'outlandish' natural and man-made objects that were brought home from voyages to distant places. Shortage of space led to a decision in 1952, in line with a number of other museums, to keep only what related to the life and history of the neighbourhood. A rare survivor is a giant tortoise given to Sir Marston Logan of Gatehouse when he was Governor of the Seychelles. Meanwhile the skeleton of an elephant, which used to be a favourite at Kirkcudbright, has now found its way to the **Royal Museum of Scotland**.

Displays and collections in this delightful museum are old fashioned. Their virtue is the endless variety of things to look at, things for the imagination to work on. No doubt much needs to be done to ensure that the objects are not allowed to deteriorate, but this can be done without disturbing the essential character of the place.

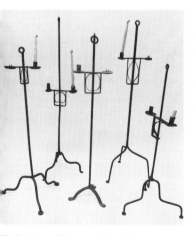

'Carles' (wrought iron candlesticks)

MEIGLE (T)

Meigle Sculptured Stones

Meigle, Perthshire   (031) 244 3101
Closed Sundays. 🅢
& S: steps up to building
🏛 & 👫 book in advance by
telephone: (031) 244 3087.

The approach to the museum is unimpressive. It is an old stone schoolhouse beside the church, and you may well have to go to a private house to rouse the custodian. Inside, the presentation has a presbyterian starkness – plain timber roof, white walls, green lino floor. Yet here is an assembly of some thirty early Christian and Pictish stone monuments which come from the immediate vicinity. They are among over 500 carved stones still surviving from the early Christian period in Scotland. Many of them are in Fife and Tayside, a good many still standing in their original locations and now in the care of the Ancient Monuments section of the Scottish Development Department. Other important collections, which like Meigle are also in their care, are in the museums at *Whithorn Cathedral Priory, St Andrews Cathedral* and *St Vigeans, Arbroath.*

The majority of the stones in this collection are either gravestones that would have been placed horizontally, or cross-slabs (i.e. stone blocks carrying the symbol of the cross) that were originally standing. They are dated to between the 8th and 10th centuries AD.

The centrepiece of this display is a stone of heroic proportions, almost seven feet high and very broad. On one side is carved Daniel surrounded by four fierce lions, with an equestrian group above and a centaur, a dragon and other figures beneath. On the other side are three pairs of beasts facing each other, and these are surmounted by a great 'ring of glory' as it is called, a wheel containing a cross carved and decorated in high relief.

This is made all the more impressive because the sculptors deliberately chose a block of sandstone in which the normal dark red colour gives way to a pale grey at the place where the ring of glory begins, as though the stone itself had become sanctified by the sacred symbol.

The equestrian groups testify to the fact that this was a society that set great store by their horses. More than this, the images of horses that have been best preserved make us aware that the sculptors had a sure sense of grandeur and monumentality in their design and a very sophisticated sense of shape in

The great cross slab (no. 2)

General view of the display

MINTLAW (G)
North East of Scotland Agricultural Heritage Centre

Aden Country Park, Mintlaw, by Peterhead AB4 8LD   (0771) 22857
Open daily May to September, and weekends during October and April. F ▣ P ⬤ W
♿ & ♿ welcome but must book in advance; admission in closed season by prior arrangement. District Ranger Service and Wildlife Centre. Caravan site open April to September.

Aden was a farming estate that was owned by the Russell family from 1758 to 1937. Thereafter the building began to fall into decay, until the estate was taken over in the 1970s by the District Council, who have restored the Home Farm and are administering the whole estate as a country park for the use of the general public. The Heritage Centre is concerned with agriculture in North-East Scotland, and functions partly as a centre for continuing research on the subject.

The Home Farm is a unique semi-circular steading built about 1800 (it seems to have been intended as a full circle), with a dovecote or 'doocot' as its central feature. The visitor enters by the doocot. The nesting boxes for the doves are exposed overhead, although originally there was a floor in between providing a 'chamber' or room where the unmarried farm servants slept during their six-month term of employment.

One quadrant of the semi-circle takes you through a simple but unexpectedly evocative series of statements based on accounts of some of the workers on the farm, describing the daily lives of the people who performed its various duties – the dairymaid, the cow bailie, the horseman and so on. Further on is the two-room dwelling of Jimmy Thomson the horseman, where you are likely to meet a lady baking the

their execution. Furthermore, these representations are a result of acute observation, which even provides evidence of the horsemanship of the men represented.

Meigle lies right in the middle of the long band of fertile, flat ground in the Tay valley, Strathmore, between the Sidlaw hills on the south and the mass of the Highlands to the north. From the Pictish stones assembled here, and others still standing further up the valley, archaeologists have drawn the conclusion that Meigle must have been an ecclesiastical centre, which attracted important secular burials. In support of this theory, Thana, who was perhaps a

monastic annalist, is recorded as working at Meigle in the mid-9th century.

For the ordinary visitor, the very unimpressiveness of the neighbourhood is an important element in the experience of seeing these stones. In this situation, the 'ring of glory' is unforgettable, even when you have to get a key to go indoors to see it. All sorts of simple, earthy questions about the circumstances of this civilisation are raised in our minds from seeing the stones in their original environment, whatever other questions are prompted by seeing similar stones from a wider range of localities in a large central museum.

raditional form of scones or oatcakes
or you.

Upstairs is an area used for tempor-
ry exhibitions. In 1987–88 it housed a
eries of photographs of farmhands
nd others from before 1914, lent by
he Buchan Heritage Society. At this
listance in time, we are often struck
nore forcibly by the formality of these
ccasions, and by the awkward looks
nd attitudes of these men and women
s they stand in front of the camera,
mpatient to get back to more familiar
hings, than by anything we learn of
heir daily lives.

The main exhibition, called 'Weel
rocht Grun' (well worked ground) is
n a big hangar at the back of the
teading. The early part illustrates the
rimitive operations involved in estab-
shing farmland: clearing the land of
tones, draining it and fencing it to
eparate livestock from crops, and the
riginal method of ploughing with six
airs of oxen. This is fascinating, the
tory is peculiarly that of the North
Cast of Scotland, and the wall texts are
lesigned to allow visitors to take in
nformation at three levels, according
o the time they have or their degree of
nterest.

Visitors are then led through a large

The steading with its central dovecote

space that has recently been laid out as
a permanent exhibition, expertly
mounted using all the advantages of
modern display techniques. Here the
gradual development of farming
methods, and the tools and machines
that were invented to reduce the back-
breaking labour involved in farming,
are presented chronologically. A farm-
yard atmosphere is generated by a
tape-recording of clucking, crowing,
clopping, whinnying and occasional
traditional ditties. The visitor from the
south will not understand all the words
he hears or sees quoted on the walls,
but the language is quite properly seen

as an essential part of the tradition.
The implements are taken from the
collection of Hew McCall Smith of
Adamston, Huntly, which was acquired by the District Council in 1983.

We meet here one of the problems
of communication which are perhaps
insoluble. The display makes perfect
good sense, and fulfils its purpose in an
exemplary way, for someone brought
up in the North East. However, for
those of us who come from outside the
area, the more the mechanisation of
farming moves into the age of the
combine harvester and the Fordson
tractor (they are both present here), the
less distinctive it is to this part of
Scotland. To this extent we could be
seeing the same display demonstrating
the same developments anywhere from
Manitoba to Georgia. It is because of
this that the early phase of the exhibition and the accounts of the farm
workers on the estate are so rewarding,
not only for local people. These also
deal with problems or a way of life
common to many areas, but are seen
under the particular aspect that presented itself in this part of Europe.
They retain a local accent, like the
language itself.

The exhibition is accompanied by an
authoritative booklet, 'North East
Farming Life'. At the end of the display there is an excellent ten-minute
video in cartoon form, 'The Shape of
the Present', which outlines – accur-
ately but irreverently – the history of
land use in the North East from intractable wilderness to . . . theme park
(you may have to ask for it specially).

isitors to the 'Weel vrocht grun' display

MONTROSE (T)

Montrose Museum & Art Gallery

Panmure Place, Montrose
DD10 8HE   (0674) 73232
Closed Sundays September to
June. ⬛
&: first floor inaccessible to
wheelchairs.
⬛ & ⬛ welcome but must book in
advance.

Montrose is among Scotland's oldest
museums. The Montrose Natural History
and Antiquarian Society was
founded in 1837. The museum itself,
which presents a neatly symmetrical
classical façade to the street, was purpose
built and opened in 1842. The
main area inside follows the accepted
pattern of the time, with top-lighting in
a coved ceiling and a gallery at first
floor level with an ironwork balustrade,
which is wide enough to accommodate
showcases.

Perhaps the most valued exhibit is
the Inchbrayock, or so-called Samson
stone, a Pictish stone of 850–950 AD
with a Christian cross on one side, and
on the reverse a nobleman hunting
with horse, spear, sword, shield and
deerhound, and Samson slaying the
Philistine with a jawbone of disproportionate
size. It is one of three carved
stones found in the middle of the 19th
century on a little island in the main
channel of the River Esk, which had a
small church on it.

The displays in the main area downstairs
are arranged in a series of showcases
devoted to different themes.
From the display on the Jacobites we
learn that Montrose strongly supported
the Stuarts, and the Jacobites occupied
the town at one stage. Later Montrose
history includes a splendid weathercock
in beaten metal (in the form of a
cock of course) and a communion plate
from Montrose old parish church of
impressive size. Like a number of other
Scottish towns, Montrose had its silversmiths,
and the collection includes a
beautiful communion cup of 1688
from Laurencekirk Parish Church.
Other displays celebrate the Montrose

makers of stone and glass bottles,
James Marquis of Montrose; the
Dryleys Pottery and Tile Works, which
produced simple brown and cream
slipware dishes in the first half of the
19th century; the local regiments; and
the Provost's regalia.

Montrose is one of the museums
that, from its age, we should expect to
have an ethnographical collection. And
so indeed it did, but unhappily a decision
was taken since the last war, as it
was in a number of other Scottish
museums, to get rid of most of the
things that were not of strictly local
interest. A remnant was allowed to
survive and in 1988, in honour of
celebrations of Australia, there was a
display of Australian Aboriginal and
wild life. The first travellers from
Angus to Australia were missionaries
and seamen. Among the gifts to the
museum from these travels are shells
from Australian beaches collected at
Port Jackson near Botany Bay by the
Hon. James Inglis of Montrose, who
rose to become the Australian Minister
for Public Instruction and gave them to
the museum in 1887.

An extension room at the back is
used mainly for the display of art.
Besides portraits by Chalmers, a native
of Montrose, the most interesting pictures
are a group of topographical
views. Especially noteworthy is a depiction
of Montrose High Street with
figures of the residents arrayed in the
foreground, painted by a Montrose
schoolmaster in 1826.

The gallery upstairs is devoted to
maritime history and related trades, so
that fishing, shipbuilding and whaling
(there were two whaling companies in
Montrose) take pride of place. Perhaps
perversely, three things remain in my
mind. One is the trade between Montrose
and the Baltic – there is a primitive
picture of the 'Clio' from Montrose
at Riga in 1880. Another is a
large model of a British man-of-war
made out of bone with exceptional
craftsmanship by Napoleonic prisoners
at Portsmouth. It is here because the
nephew of the man who bought it in
Portsmouth gave it to the museum in
1897. The third thing is a wretched
fragment of paper written in pencil

Alexander Milne, Montrose High Street, *1826*

The Inchbrayock stone

which was in a bottle picked up at sea by fishermen from nearby Ferryden in 1857. It had been written by the chief mate of the brig 'Ellen' of Whitby eighty years before: 'Blowing a hurricane lying to with close-reefed main topsails ship waterlogged. Cargo of wood from Quebec. No water on board, provisions all gone. Eat the dog yesterday. Three men left alive. Lord have mercy on our souls. Amen.'

Leading off the gallery, in the extension building, is a display of natural history. It is arranged conventionally, with showcases devoted to seaside, the town, farmland, woodland, freshwater, estuary, but it is one of the livelier natural history displays in museums of this size and, with good descriptive labels discreetly at hand, one of the more interesting. It deals only with the district around Montrose, but the range is very wide, from seals and deer to golden eagles and pink-footed geese. Other cases are reserved for agates, for which Montrose is well known, and old red sandstone fossils (with notes on two distinguished Victorian geologists of Angus, Hugh Mitchell and Dr J.C. Howden).

NAIRN (H)

Nairn Literary Institute Museum

Viewfield House, King Street, Nairn
Closed October to May, otherwise closed Sundays. 🄵 🄿
&: inaccessible to wheelchairs.
🛈 & ♟ must book with Mrs P.J. Hossack, Honorary Curator, 60 Wyris Drive, Achareidh, Nairn (0667) 55100

One way to preserve things for future generations is to shut them away in whisky cases. It is our good fortune that this is what happened to the ethnographical collections of the Nairn Literary Institute, during the fashion for throwing out everything except items of strictly local history; the things that had been brought back by seamen and other travellers from Nairn were allowed to survive. The collection was started by the Nairn Literary Society in 1858, and was housed in a room on the High Street. The displays have recently been reorganised on the first floor of what was once a private house with a reticent classical façade. The Society's first Chairman, Dr John Grigor, stands proudly on his pedestal in front in a soft brimmed hat.

This is not the place to find the latest in showcase design or the most up-to-date museum display techniques. The collection was born of enthusiasm, and equally its revival and maintenance now rely on the enthusiasm of volunteers, who cherish the museum as something that has had, and continues to have, a valuable place in the cultural life of Nairn, and who now accept the history of the museum itself and its activators as part of their heritage.

Although the founding society was a 'literary' one, at least in name, the interests of members took them out on expeditions into the countryside round Nairn, and the early collections included fossils and minerals, which

Peruvian double-bodied vessel

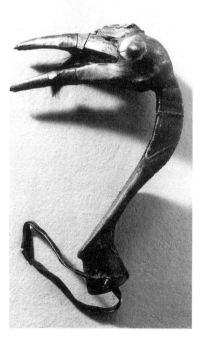

Hornbill decoy

Victorian shell frames

NEW ABBEY (D)

Shambellie House Museum of Costume

New Abbey, Dumfriesshire
(038 785) 375
Closed October to April, otherwise closed Fridays and Saturdays. **F**
P &. S
M̶ & **Ṫ** welcome but must book in advance through Royal Museum of Scotland (031) 225 7534

Shambellie House is approached on foot up a pleasantly wooded driveway (the word 'up' is meaningful here). It is worth visiting for two quite separate reasons: the house itself and the display of costume. The house was built by David Bryce in 1856 for William Stewart of Shambellie, a minor Scottish landowner whose roots in Galloway went back to the early years of the

would normally be counted as 'philosophical' (i.e. concerned with the natural sciences). Evidently, too, ethnography was always a priority.

The first acquisition was a gift in 1858 of 'A young rattlesnake taken by the late Major Grant of Auchindowne from the back settlement of America about 1800.' This was followed by a group of clubs from Fiji in 1863, a turtle in 1879, a beautiful hornbill decoy, several pieces of Peruvian pottery, and things from Nigeria, Australia and the Far East. The most popular exhibit for the many schoolchildren who now visit the museum is the shrunken head from Borneo. (Children visiting the museum at **Elgin** are reported to share this predilection.) These are among the things now exhibited in a room devoted to 'The Nairn Explorers'. Principal among them was James Augustus Grant (1827–92), a son of the Nairn manse who began his explorations in India and later joined his contemporary John Speke, who discovered the source of the Nile. Other early gifts to the natural history collec-

tion included shark's teeth, three sawfish, a group of Australian shells, and such curiosities as an elephant's toenail.

Of particular interest now are the fossils that were collected in the neighbourhood of Nairn in the 1830s by a factor of the Earl of Cawdor, William Stables, which were given to the Institute by Lord Cawdor in 1884.

All these things have been in the museum for over a hundred years. They are arranged in a display on 'The Natural Scene', which also includes a fairly extensive collection of geological samples given in 1902.

The literary society's members also concerned themselves with the history of their own district, an interest that is kept alive by the present curator. Old Nairn, in the Victorian era particularly, is recalled in the display 'Another way of life'. Particularly good is the collection of old photographs of houses and people in the district. Many of these are put together with old press cuttings and other accounts in albums, which the visitor is left free to look through.

Evening dresses, c.1913–14

Day dresses of c. 1860–1871

15th century. Only three rooms are open to the public, which means that at popular times they tend to become overcrowded. The visitor is led through them between ropes, and on either side are arrangements of mannequins, which strike a happy balance between the wooden and the over-realistic. The groups of figures make sense together and are well adapted to the spaces they are made to occupy in the rooms.

The costume displays are changed each season. When I visited, a dazzling selection of 31 costumes were on show (from a total collection of over 2000), each one a work of art in its own right. These were aristocrats of dress, beautifully made of the most exquisite materials, an analogy to the aristocrats of the motor car in **Doune Motor Museum**.

There was, besides, an engagingly personal touch, for instance in the inclusion of a display of historical fancy dress, unexpected in museums of costume and in this case a product of the enthusiasm of the man who arranged it

Fancy dress

– Charles Stewart, a descendant of the man who had the house built. It was Charles Stewart who made the collection of costume, and gave both the house and the collection in 1977 to the **Royal Scottish Museum** as it then was, to form the national collection of costume for Scotland.

The quality of the costumes on show suggests that the whole collection is on a very high level, which augurs well for the quality of future displays. Yet it is a lot to ask that the personal touch marking a display by the collector himself should be matched by a museum curator, however knowledgeable and perceptive.

No additions are made to the collection at Shambellie, but it is supplemented as a national collection by costumes in the National Museums, which were already fairly extensive before Charles Stewart's gift. A limitation of Shambellie is that there is so far no one in the building who is able to answer questions about the collection and, although the costumes are all housed there, arrangements for interested visitors to see any in reserve have to be made at the **Royal Museum of Scotland** in Edinburgh. Where such a small proportion of the whole collection is on show at any one time, this is a serious drawback.

If this is the drawback of a branch museum so far from its base, there are solid advantages in its being under the protection of a national institution. Warding and presentation are of a standard that few locally-funded museums can match, and the standard of photography and publication is high.

Publications include a first class booklet on the history of the house by Alistair Rowan, who had made a special study of the architect William Bryce and was considerably abetted by a fairly extensive documentation of the commission, the building itself and its owners. The booklet is well illustrated, in part by Charles Stewart himself. It was Mr Stewart's work as an illustrator that first inspired him to collect historical costume, and a second illustrated booklet is available in which he gives a very lively and readable account of the way he formed his collection.

NEWTONGRANGE

(L)

Scottish Mining Museum (Newtongrange)

Lady Victoria Colliery, Newtongrange, Midlothian EH22 4QN (031) 663 7519
Closed Mondays. 🚻 🎦 🅿
♿ S: inaccessible to wheelchairs and difficult for disabled, except for restaurant.
🏫 & 🍴 welcome but must book in advance.

The Lady Victoria Colliery was built at the end of the last century, and from the start it was seen as the jewel in the crown of Scottish coalfields. Owned by the Marquess of Lothian, it was one of the most advanced coal mines of its period, and when it went out of operation in 1981 had pioneered many new techniques in the working of coal.

An imaginative negotiation, which involved Lothian Regional Council and the District Councils of Midlothian and East Lothian, brought a trust into being to form the Scottish Mining Museum, based partly at Newtongrange and partly at *Prestongrange*, Prestonpans, one of the oldest coal mining sites in Scotland on the Firth of Forth 8 miles to the north.

The visitor to Newtongrange is introduced to the life of the coal company as it was when the colliery was comparatively new, in the 1890s. At the beginning is a sequence of six life-size tableaux, each of which is accompanied by a dramatic dialogue on tape. This is of an exceptionally high standard. The home life of the miner and the decision-making processes of the mine owner, the manager and the board are vividly presented. It is not a particularly nostalgic view of the past.

The visit to the mine itself takes the form of a guided tour. Considerations of safety make this unavoidable, not only for the considerable number of school parties that visit the museum.

Lady Victoria Colliery

The winding engine

The first item we see is the enormous winding engine that moved the cages up and down the mineshaft. The engine, which was steam driven, has been made to operate electrically, sometimes with visitors at the controls so that they get a taste of the responsibility held by the driver, on whom the safety – and even the lives – of the men depended.

The next stage is the ground-level structures of the mine itself, at the head of the pitshaft, where the men went down to work. The coal was brought up in the mineshaft cages in tubs which were turned round here and sent up a ramp to be discharged onto a moving belt below, where an army of women sorted the coal. Although in fact so little of the reality of the working of the mine survives, we receive a considerable impression from the sheer size of the buildings and, if the tubs are set going, the continuous roar and clatter of the machinery.

The pitshaft has been filled in for safety reasons, but plans are in hand for an 'underground experience', by which a realistic idea of the working conditions in the pit can be recreated.

But even without this Newtongrange has much to offer the visitor. We are at a coal mine, which most of us had little chance of seeing while it was in production. It is now deserted, and the very vastness and emptiness of the place brings home something of what was involved in this giant industry when it was at its height, and what is involved now in its recession.

The museum also acts as a focus for the past history of the area, not just the mine itself. The town of Newtongrange was built for the miners and their families, and many of them still live there. So while the exhibition area and the collections of the museum relate mainly to the technology of mining, a number of leaflets have been produced that record aspects of the social life of the miners and their families, and the conditions in which they lived. In addition, fulfilling its role as the national centre for research and information on coal mining in Scotland, the museum is actively engaged in collecting evidence about the industry before it disappears.

PAISLEY (S)

Paisley Museum & Art Gallery

*High Street, Paisley, Renfrewshire
PA1 2BA　　(041) 889 3151*
Closed Sundays. ▣　&
♿ & ♿ welcome but must book in advance.

The museum and library at Paisley are housed in a handsome classical building in pale orange sandstone, which stands directly on the High Street, a symbol of its importance to the town when it was built in 1870 and of the town's prosperity then. A painting of Paisley Cross by James Christie, with ranks of merchants, businessmen, bankers, engineers and artists, reveals a typical prosperous Victorian town towards the end of the 19th century.

The impetus for creating the museum came from the Paisley Philosophical Society. The money came from the Coats family, of the famous thread firm of J. & P. Coats. Responsibility for maintenance was accepted by Paisley Town Council, which thus became the first municipal authority to run a museum in Scotland. Sir Peter Coats and other members of the family have been strong supporters and benefactors of the museum, giving not only

Illuminated initial from the Arbuthnot missal

funds but some of the most precious exhibits as well. These include a copy of Audubon's *Birds of North America* and some beautiful illuminated manuscripts, most notably the Arbuthnott Missal, Horae and Psalter, the only pre-Reformation service books that have survived in Scotland.

The visitor goes upstairs to a spacious top-lit hall with a gallery at first floor level, which is now devoted to Paisley local history. A second flight of stairs brings him to a rotunda which leads into the other galleries.

Special features of Paisley's history are her industries, with household names like Robertson's marmalade, Coats sewing thread, Brown and Polson self-raising flour. There are notes here, too, on shipbuilding, and on the weaving trade which was active from the 18th century. Individual exhibits include some lovely church pewter of the kind quite often seen in Scotland's museums, and a curious weathercock from Paisley's first hospital established in 1618; and there is a celebration of Robert Tannahill, a late 18th century weaver poet who was the first secretary of the Paisley Burns Appreciation Society. Separate themes are treated in small cases offset against each other and – in keeping with current museum trends – a restricted number of exhibits (perhaps sometimes too restricted) is accompanied by explanatory texts and illustrations.

Upstairs there is an extensive natural history display, which gives the impression that this is at present one of the most active interests of the museum. (In fact, much of it had to be renewed after the war, when many of the natural history specimens were found to be in such bad condition that they were destroyed.) The first things to meet you are invitations to young people to join the nature society, a noticeboard carrying press cuttings and notes about nature conservation, an observation case (which on my visit contained Indian stick insects), and a note encouraging you to ask members of the staff for more information.

On one side are seals, lions, casts of important fossils and a huge model head of a triceratops, which are de-

Detail of a shawl, 1810–20

Bill McNamara, Handbuilt stoneware form, 1982

signed to acquaint the visitor with aspects of the earth at distant times and places. The other side is devoted to the natural history of Renfrewshire. Among quite a profusion of things, there is a good collection of insects and unpolished local minerals. It is no doubt right to treat these as 'specimens', and the information about them is good and well presented. Many of them are in fact things of intrinsic beauty, and the visitor must overlook backgrounds and labels in order to see their delicacy and intricacy.

Beyond the natural history section is an extension, opened in 1974, which houses an excellent account of the Paisley weavers and the history of the Paisley shawl in particular. There is the development of the characteristic designs, which were inspired by patterns brought from Kashmir around the beginning of the last century. Then there is the splendid ebullience of shawls made in the 1860s and 1870s (colour plate 8). The often superbly grand and beautiful colour schemes of some of the big plaids we see here must surely account to a great extent for their universal popularity. The display ends with the banner of the weavers' union, a collective that was an effective force as early as 1809 (we learn from the **People's Palace** in **Glasgow** about the Calton weavers' strike of 1787), and a celebration of Robert Cochran, one of the leaders of the movement.

The art collection consists of some 1,500 works, the nucleus of which was formed by the Paisley Art Institute. A Paisley artist that is well represented is John Henning (1771–1851), who made a considerable reputation with miniature medallion portraits in low relief. The paintings in the collection date mainly from the 19th century. Scottish artists include for example David Roberts, Sir John Lavery and E.A. Walton. French artists are mostly those who preceded Impressionism like Boudin, Fantin Latour, Monticelli and painters of the Barbizon school. Acquisitions continue to be made.

The museum has produced good illustrated booklets quite recently, one on the museum itself, and 'Why Paisley?' on the history of the Paisley shawl.

PERTH (T)

Perth Museum & Art Gallery

George Street, Perth PH1 5LB
(0738) 32488
Closed Sundays. ☐
&: Upper Rotunda and Sculpture Court inaccessible to wheelchairs; T. ⚇ & ⚉ welcome; for talks or a guide, book in advance with Education Officer.

The original museum stands out as a white domed and pedimented building of 1824, looking rather as if it had found some difficulty in squeezing itself in among its neighbours, and proclaiming in large Roman letters across its frieze not the purpose of the building but the gratitude of the citizenry to one of their principal benefactors: 'T.H. MARSHALL CIVES GRATI.' This was the subscription library and the Literary and Antiquarian Museum (it is the oldest museum building in Scotland). The extension to the left was in fact added in 1935, and at that stage the collection of the Perthshire Society of Natural Science was brought over from a different building, bringing to an amicable end an old tradition of rivalry between the two bodies.

We enter by a well-lit hall, and in front of us is an attractive glimpse

Alexander Runciman, 11th Earl of Buchan

through archways to one of the main galleries of the museum. While still in the hall, we are offered a straightforward display showing the shape of the museum and what is currently on show – the exhibits are changed at intervals, most of them drawn from the permanent collection. There is also an account of what the museum and its staff do, with an emphasis on involving visitors in an understanding and enjoyment of the heritage of Perth and Kinross. Visitors from outside Perth are made aware of the importance of residents in the active life of the museum.

The old room of the natural history collections comes as something of a shock: when I visited in 1988 it still had its black stained showcases with geological samples, birds' eggs and stuffed creatures from all countries, a human skeleton and the cast of a skull from Cromagnon. [This gallery has now been demolished. Ed.] Whether its passing is to be regretted or not, a new exhibition is due to replace it in May 1991 on the human history of the district from the early settlements to the present.

Next door is a display completed in 1985, which gives a foretaste of what we may expect. This is an impressive and intelligently planned natural history display, with a nicely judged balance between broad general information, for instance on land formation and wildlife, and specific details about what is to be found in Perth and Kinross, like the fragments of the Strathmore meteorite that fell in 1917, or the osprey, shown in a special enclosure as befits its protected status. And wherever practical there is a blessed lack of protective glass. Where one visitor may miss the chance to make exciting isolated discoveries of his own, as was possible with the old-style 'specimen' display, many more will gain real enlightenment about the broad scene and the way Perthshire fits into it.

Other sections of the museum were in 1988 devoted to furniture; the Romans in Perthshire (the find of 900,000 nails at the legionary base of Inchtuthil a little to the north has

Silver punchbowl by Robert Keay of Perth, 1817

supplied most of the museums in Britain); Pullars of Perth, the famous drycleaners; Perth glass, particularly paperweights; Perth silver, with helpful notes on other centres of silversmithing in Scotland. In the Upper Rotunda is a section on social history, which includes displays on P. Strang the chemist and other Perth shopkeepers.

Part of the legacy of the original Literary and Antiquarian Society is a fairly extensive ethnographical collection of more than 1,000 items. It has been allowed to survive in safety and a catalogue was printed recently, so that it is available to interested people. Small exhibitions drawn from the collection are put on display from time to time.

The first gift towards the art collection remains one of the most engaging of all Scottish portraits: the 11th Earl of Buchan by Alexander Runciman. Lord Buchan was instrumental in founding the Society of Antiquaries of Scotland in 1780, and he gave this portrait of himself to the Perth Literary and Antiquarian Society in 1785, soon after their foundation, 'for their place of meeting'. The main weight of the art collection is in the Scottish 19th and early 20th centuries, its nucleus being two bequests of the 1920s, by Robert Hay Robertson and a silk merchant,

Robert Brough. An active acquisitions policy is also being pursued, directed mainly at contemporary Scottish painting.

Exhibitions drawn from the permanent collection have recently been on specific themes, like an exhibition of paintings of animals during the summer of 1988. This principle has proved to be an extremely effective way of keeping interest alive in pictures, many of which are not strong enough to stand as individual masterpieces of the art. As usual, space in the museum is at a premium. An overhead grid has been introduced under the dome of the original building (very sensibly, a good photograph is shown of the earlier display there). This carries screens and cases for temporary exhibitions, which change once or twice a year. An exhibition there of Martinware pottery in the spring of 1988 was designed to encourage visitors to think about what they saw rather than merely telling them about it.

In spite of its age – and the Perth museum has a reasonable claim to be the oldest in Scotland – we are given a clear impression of a museum that is on the move, of new thinking and active research. There are likely to be new things to see by the time this guide is published.

PETERHEAD (G)

Arbuthnot Museum

St Peter Street, Peterhead AB4 6QD
(0779) 77778
Closed Sundays. ▣
&: inaccessible to wheelchairs.
▥ & ▯ welcome but must book in advance.

The Arbuthnot Museum, as its name suggests, is one of comparatively few museums in Scotland that owe their foundation, and their original collection, to a single benefactor. Adam Arbuthnot was a Peterhead merchant, born in 1773, the son of a man who had served as a Lieutenant at Culloden with the Jacobites. When he retired from business in about 1820, he turned to the collection of natural history, coins and other curiosities. There is no dividing line between a personal collection and a private museum, which Arbuthnot had thus been creating, except perhaps its availability to the public. Arbuthnot's collection was always open to anyone who wanted to visit it, and by the 1830s had become very well known in the district.

When Arbuthnot died in 1850 he left his collection to the town council of

Keith Hutton, sail maker, with his model of the 'Bendouran' now in the museum

Eskimo animal shoes, acquired in 1822

Peterhead. Some time after this, money that had been raised locally to build a worthy museum was supplemented by a grant from Andrew Carnegie to erect a public library, and in 1894 the present building, in which the two are combined, was opened.

In the meantime, in 1835, a philosophical society had been established in Peterhead, as it had in numerous other towns in Scotland from Kelso to Inverness. In the case of Peterhead it must surely have been inspired by Mr Arbuthnot's activity. Called the Peterhead Association for Science, Literature and the Arts, it too opened a museum and began to receive donations of shells, minerals and antiques. The Association lapsed for a time, was revived as the Peterhead Scientific and Literary Institute, and whatever collections survived from the two bodies were later amalgamated with the collection left by Mr Arbuthnot.

The most distinguished elements of the Arbuthnot collection are the coins and, more particularly, the artefacts made by eskimos – gloves, purses and shoes, some of them of exquisite craftsmanship. These were brought

back from whaling expeditions, and it is clear from the dates at which Arbuthnot acquired them that he got them from men with whom he had had business connections before he retired. Indeed, it seems likely that he was already asking them to look out for things and collecting them, well before he actually retired. So while these things are unusual enough in themselves as the work of eskimos, it takes an effort to keep in mind the fact that they were made anything up to 180 years ago.

Whaling is celebrated as well as fishing and boat building, which have been staples of Peterhead since the late 18th century and are still thriving. Peterhead has in fact now overtaken Aberdeen as Scotland's busiest white fish port. Particularly notable are some beautiful ship models.

In another room are displays on weaving, cooperage and – perhaps more interesting because it is hardly duplicated elsewhere – on the quarrying and working of that most durable but intractable of building materials, the granite with which so much of Aberdeenshire architecture is built.

An important element of the museum's activity stems from its role as the headquarters of the North East of Scotland Museums Service, which supports museums in *Banff, Banchory, Huntly, Inverurie* and *Stonehaven*. This leads to a considerable emphasis on the arrangement of small temporary exhibitions that can be sent on tour. Exhibitions are arranged in house, in collaboration with organisations like the Peacock Printmakers in Aberdeen or the Scottish Sculpture Workshop at Lumsden, or brought in from elsewhere. One of the main rooms of the museum is reserved for temporary exhibitions of this kind.

An interesting feature, devised originally by the Scottish Arts Council and first taken up at Peterhead, is the 'book table'. The pages of the 'books' are protected by plastic and are large enough to carry original lithographs or drawings. The 'books' are usually commissioned from artists, and may contain some thirty pages. Their security is, so to speak, built in, so that the range of places where they can go is extended to include small libraries and other places not served by museums. It can indeed be said that they are much better suited to these smaller places, since only one or two people at a time can look at them.

Visitors at the book table

RUTHWELL (D)

Savings Banks Museum

Ruthwell, Dumfriesshire DG1 4NN
(0387) 87640
Closed Sundays and Mondays
October to March. 🅵 ♿
♿ & 👥 welcome but must book in
advance

This museum lies rather out of the way and consists of one not very large room in a cottage, whose original character is partially hidden by screens, cases and wall panels used to accommodate the objects, photographs and other exhibits in the display. And quite a lot depends, given the nature of the subject, on written description. So there would seem to be little to lose in giving it a miss. But if you do, you miss the story of one of Scotland's most remarkable men, and there is no other way of discovering the measure of his greatness than by standing in the flat, isolated and unpromising countryside where he worked. It is a story of unshakeable moral integrity, intellectual curiosity, compassion for the underprivileged, brilliant managerial skills, a gift for teaching and publicising, a fluent pen and tireless energy, all concentrated in a single man.

The man was the Rev Dr Henry Duncan, Minister of Ruthwell. Born in 1774, he was a contemporary of Walter

From a portrait of Henry Duncan

Scott, and Carlyle called him 'the amiablest and kindliest of men'. In 1839 he was made Moderator of the General Assembly of the Church of Scotland. Four years later, at the Disruption of the established church, he was among the many ministers who walked out to become ministers of the Free Church. For Duncan this meant not only giving up the manse and his living, but an end to a life's work in his parish.

One of his major achievements, and the reason for the museum, was to

The museum seen from the road

found the savings movement in Britain. The cottage had been the venue of the Ruthwell Friendly Society, which Duncan revived in 1800. The Friendly Society offered a realistic form of insurance for working men in the Napoleonic era, when their livelihood had become precarious, providing sickness, unemployment and other benefits to those who had been members for at least three years. In 1810 Duncan founded a Savings Bank, where an account could be opened with sixpence at a time when the regular banks would accept no accounts of less than £10. Once it was started at Ruthwell, Duncan spent much of his time – and latterly a large part of his stipend in postage – in promoting the movement throughout Britain.

He was noted for his talents as a writer and preacher. He was a skilled draughtsman, and examples of his drawings are to be seen here. He started two local newspapers, which were largely written by himself, in order to keep his parishioners in touch with world events.

He also took an active interest, like a number of his contemporaries elsewhere in Scotland, in the geology of his area. A slab of red sandstone from the Corncockle Muir quarry, which had a set of footprints on it, led him in 1824 to write the first scientific study of fossil footprints to be published in Britain.

A visit to Ruthwell must include the whitewashed church with its overcrowded graveyard, because this is where the Ruthwell Cross, one of the primary relics of Christianity in Scotland, is housed. Rather strangely, although the church has a plaque dedicated to the memory of Henry Duncan as its minister, and plenty of information about the history of the cross, little reference is made to Duncan's share in it.

In fact it was Duncan who retrieved all that could be found of the cross from where it lay, buried in the churchyard. He reassembled it with considerable scholarship, although admittedly he got one of the stone sections the wrong way round. He then re-erected it in the garden of his man-

The Ruthwell Cross

se. Finding that the short transverse arm of the cross was missing, Duncan got a local stonemason to replace it with one of his own design. It may be hard for us to excuse such a thorough scholar for this act, which would be unthinkable now. However it was probably just as hard for Duncan to excuse the destruction of the cross by the image-breakers of the Reformation, who were after all scarcely further away from him in time than he is from ourselves.

The museum was established by TSB Association and is administered by them in honour of their founder. A very well-produced folder on Duncan's history, 'The Ruthwell Connection', is available, and the curator is an enthusiast who is ready to answer your questions.

SELKIRK (B)

Halliwell's House & Robson Gallery

Halliwell's Close, Market Place, Selkirk TD7 4AE   (0750) 20096
Closed Sunday mornings. 🅐 🅿
&: wheelchair access to ground floor only.
🚻 & 🚻 welcome but must book in advance; reduced prices.

Halliwell's House stands in a picturesque old close. House and close both take their name from an early 18th century wigmaker who lived there. The present building dates from about 1800, but it is still the oldest dwelling in Selkirk.

A hardware business was started in the house early in the 19th century. The last man to run the business, Fred Robson, also began to collect domestic hardware, and in 1956 he opened a Museum of Old Ironmongery there. In 1984 the building was restored and partly reconstructed. The ironmongery remains the dominant feature of the ground floor, which it now shares with the Tourist Information Centre. The museum section on the first floor is devoted to the history of Selkirk, and there is also the Robson Gallery, reserved for a regular programme of temporary exhibitions, a fair proportion of which are devised in the museum itself rather than being brought on loan from elsewhere.

The reconstruction of the ironmongery shop is extremely attractive, complete up to the rafters and down to the creaking wooden floor. The wares on show are those that would have been on offer around the end of the last century, including guns, doorknockers, goffering irons, shoelaces, butter pats, whale oil, an early pressure cooker, an impressive array of oil lamps, and many other things besides.

The presentation includes a consideration of the kind of people that were the customers of an ironmongery business in a Borders market town of the

The ironmonger's shop

Edwardian age. There is a taped dramatisation of typical discussions between the ironmonger and his customers. Meanwhile the visitor is free to walk into the shop – on the customers' side of the counter, of course – and on occasions when there are school parties the role of the shopkeeper may be re-enacted for them.

The staircase to the first floor is part of the modern adaptation. This is made clear – no doubt deliberately – by the obtrusive acid-green colour of the treads and handrail.

Upstairs one of the exhibits on the history of Selkirk is the tattered remnants of a banner, which is traditionally described as an English flag captured by men of Selkirk in 1513 at the disastrous battle of Flodden Field, some thirty miles to the east. (There seems no reason to disbelieve this tradition, even if there is little chance of proving it.) However this may be, the status of Selkirk as a Royal Burgh was confirmed soon afterwards, and its charter specified the burghers' right to hold and defend their extensive common lands. From this originated the colourful ceremony of the Selkirk Common Riding, whereby the legitimate boundaries of the lands were reasserted each year to prevent their encroachment by neighbouring landowners.

In course of time the craftsmen of the town formed themselves into guilds, as they did elsewhere, including weavers, tailors, shoemakers, hammermen and fleshers (butchers). Some still survive, and there is a display of their emblems, banners and drums, which came to feature in the Common Riding.

The museum has two short videos of the Common Riding, which remains an important annual event in the town. They incorporate old film footage of earlier occasions, and give a vivid impression of the performance and the astonishing crowds it attracts each year.

There is a good guide to the museum, and a number of leaflets on the building and on the ironmongery business which are aimed at younger visitors.

STIRLING (C)

The Smith Art Gallery & Museum

40 Albert Place, Dumbarton Road, Stirling FK8 2RQ   (0786) 71917
Closed Mondays. **F**   **W**

Children visiting a temporary exhibition in 1988

The visitor enters a somewhat unpromising Victorian building by a pedimented façade with some obscure devices on the tympanum now abraded by the weather, and comes unexpectedly upon a long, narrow vista running right through the building, which is white, bright and welcoming. This symbolises the history of the museum, from the unusual circumstances of its foundation through a period of delapidation and decay to its presence vigorous revival.

The founder, Thomas Stuart Smith, was evidently descended from the Stuarts of Glassingall, an estate near Dunblane. He seems by nature to have been a dilettante of the old school, who spent much of his time in Italy, collecting pictures and working as a painter himself. (His own work, at least what we see of it in the museum, is unremarkable.) In 1856 he fell heir to Glassingall, but found himself ill-suited to the life and work of a laird, and was glad to sell the estate and retire to London.

Cast of the Stirling burgh seal

He seems however to have retained either an affection for Stirling or a sense of obligation towards the town, and when he died in 1869 he left to Stirling his collection of paintings, by himself and other artists, and an endowment for a museum, which was built five years later. The Trustees decided that part of the endowment should go towards acquiring a collection that was to illustrate Stirling and its neighbourhood, and to a lesser extent Scotland, with objects from further afield included for comparison.

By the 1950s the endowment had become totally inadequate to maintain the museum, and it was doubtful whether it had any future. A group of Friends of the Museum, started in about 1970, prevented the complete closure of the museum when the building was closed for renovation. A new committee was formed in 1973, principally through the support of Stirling District Council and Central Regional Council. There is now a permanent staff, actively engaged in finding the means to put the building and its collections to rights, and at the same time pursuing a lively policy aimed at generating interest and a firm nucleus of support from people in the neighbourhood by producing a regular series of publications, temporary exhibitions, performances and other events.

The present plan reserves the biggest of the spaces available for temporary exhibitions. Opened in 1987, this space is an attractively straightforward and unpretentious restoration which makes no attempt to hide the articulation of the roof. Regular features are the Stirling Biennial art exhibition and the Primary Children's Art Exhibition. There will also be a room with changing exhibitions of local interest, a bookshop and a small cafeteria. [All open 1989. Ed.]

Meanwhile the permanent collection is not forgotten. A substantial catalogue, published in 1934, gives some idea of its range: paintings, natural history, archaeology, a Scottish historical collection of considerable distinction, and a fairly strong military collection, especially of arms and armour. And among instruments of torture deposited by the Town Council when they were no longer in use is 'a cap of rough hair worn by Burke the body-snatcher'.

The museum's exhibition programme will now be bringing many of these things on display again. Meanwhile in 1988 the Friends had launched a public appeal, which was proving very successful, for funds to restore the best of the collection of paintings.

TAIN (H)
Tain & District Museum & Clan Ross Centre

Castle Brae, Tain IV19 1AJ
(0862) 2140
Closed October to Easter, otherwise closed Sundays. (Viewing out of season available: apply to District Office, High Street.) ⓈI but Ⓕ to OAPs and children.
&: a few steps up to the museum are difficult.
⌨ & ♦ welcome but must book in advance.

The museum is in a small but attractive 19th century building that belonged to the church and overlooks the churchyard. It is an independent museum, which means that the person looking after it when you go there is likely to be a volunteer who is genuinely interested in the history of Tain and can supplement what you learn from the exhibits and the explanations set out in the museum.

Exhibits and explanations play two rather different roles here. The displays have recently been reorganised. The showcases are well designed and make good use of the available space, which is extremely limited. Where there are no cases, there are descriptive texts mounted on the wall, well produced in readable format.

Some of these texts are valuable accounts, especially for people that live nearby and wish to understand how the administration of their parish fits into the general pattern of the times (Tain is in fact a Royal Burgh) as far as roads and communications, education, law and order, poor relief and sanitation, besides domestic life are concerned. The texts are accompanied by contemporary quotations and often by old photographs.

Some of the texts have a wider interest, when they deal with things that are distinctive to the area: the history of

One of the series of medieval wooden panels from the King's Room, Stirling Castle

Tain silver tablespoon and toddy ladles

*Leather bowl for eggs, 1873 butter clapper
and hand-moulded pottery teapot from Lewis*

county town; or the Easter Ross estates and the sad history of the 19th century 'improvements' – there is a photograph of the tragic message on the church window at Croick, inland up Strathcarron, recording the evicted families that took refuge there in 1845. It has to be said, however, that the texts are sometimes a good deal longer than most of us are prepared to read standing up, and leave the impression that the exhibits were thought of by the writer as illustrating the texts rather than the other way round.

Visitors from outside will find most of their interest in the objects themselves. There is a sense of fastidiousness with which the exhibits have been chosen, even down to items of domestic use, giving the impression that everything had to pass a test of quality or interest in order to be included. Close study is therefore likely to repay, and every visitor will find different things that take his eye.

Domestic items include for example a shallow leather bowl, perhaps for collecting eggs; an ungainly pottery teapot from Barvas on the Isle of Lewis, made in the late 19th century following a tradition of moulding by hand and then baking with burning peats inside and out; a wooden butter clapper engraved 'K.F.Mth 1873', which would have been carefully carved for the birthday of a little farm girl. Each object is accompanied by a description of this kind.

There is a small group of beautiful silver spoons that were made in Tain, which include two small sauce ladles made by Hugh Ross about 1775 with feather-edged engraving round the handle and a larger tablespoon by Alexander Stewart, one of a family of tinker silversmiths who were working in Tain around 1796–1826. A section devoted to the church has beautiful examples of pewter communion cups and plates; an unbleached linen communion cloth of the mid-19th century with lead at the corners to hold it down in the wind during outdoor services; and a 'mort bell' and old funeral bell. Up to the turn of the century deaths in Tain were intimated by the beadle (his three-cornered hat is also here), who

'Mort bell' and funerary bell

called out the name and the time of the funeral, and headed the funeral procession ringing the mort bell.

Other things of interest are a wine glass used on the coach from Inverness to Tain, which has a ball foot like a stirrup cup as it was not intended to be set down while full; a rare tool for pulling out thistles; a copper whisky still that was in use in the 1890s (presumably illegally, the first legal stills were operating around 1840). There are also sections on Ross of Pitcalnie and Clan Ross, the museum being the Clan Ross Centre, and on the local regiments and fencibles of the 18th century.

Shot flask, bullet mould and powder flask

mussel fishing from the mussel 'scalps' or beds, when mussels were used for baiting lines rather than for human consumption; notes on the Pictish stones that can be seen in the area, for instance the cross-slabs at Nigg and Shandwick; an account of the rivalry between Tain and Dingwall as to which should to be chosen as the

WANLOCKHEAD
D)

Museum of Scottish Lead Mining

Goldscaur Row, Wanlockhead, by Biggar, Lanarkshire (0659) 74387
Closed mid-October to Easter.
🅿 ♿

🍴 & 🚻 welcome, preferably book in advance.

You can't go to Wanlockhead and the neighbouring village of Leadhills, standing alone high up in the barren hills of Upper Nithsdale, without enquiring about their history. This is now available to us in the Scottish Lead Mining Museum at Wanlockhead and the Mining Trail that takes you through the village.

The museum or visitor centre itself is in the old mining forge. A seven-minute video gives an outline of the history, which begins in the 16th century when, surprisingly enough, the recovery of gold in these hills was a commercial proposition. This was followed early in the 18th century with the development of the lead mining industry which lasted until the 1950s.

There are excellent reconstructions of a mine shaft with a rag and chain pump, and the scene in a smelting works, which are based on drawings made here in the latter part of the 18th century by David Allan. There are examples of the minerals found in the area – over 60 different varieties have been identified, including galena, the mixture of silver and lead that was chiefly being quarried. There is a working model of the late 19th century water-powered beam pumping engine that survives outside, and a model of a much larger pumping engine built in 1832, which had been in use nearby until 1925 and was found 700 feet underground in an exploration as recent as 1981.

This characterises the nature of the Wanlockhead enterprise. Research is

Early photograph of lead miners

still being actively pursued, into the geology and technology of the mines and into the social history of the miners and their families. The visitor is invited to become involved in the quest, and a number of modestly produced leaflets provide him with a wealth of information.

The museum complex owes its origins to the work and enthusiasm of one man, Geoffrey Downs Rose, who settled in Wanlockhead in 1979 and be-

gan to devote himself to tracing the history of the mines, which had then only recently closed. It is now administered by the Wanlockhead Museum Trust, which is run by members of the village council.

At the highest point of the Mining Trail is the miners' library. This and the library up the road at Leadhills are two of the oldest lending libraries in Britain, opened in 1756 and 1742 respectively, the earlier one under the

Drawing of the Wanlockhead lead mines, 1775, probably by John Clerk of Eldin

The beam pumping engine

inspiration of Allan Ramsay, the poet, whose father was an overseer in the lead mines. Both libraries survive with most of their books intact.

The visitor is taken into the Loch Nell lead mine, and the guide describes some of the mineral ores in the hill. His description of mining conditions in the 18th century is enlivened by a tableau set up about a quarter of a mile into the mine. At that point a shaft drops 90 feet to mine workings lower down. The sight is unexpected and very dramatic. This part of the mine had to be closed off in 1987 for safety reasons as a result of a fall of rock, but it is planned to re-open it in 1990.

The trail leads down the course of a stream, where remnants of the old narrow gauge railway and its trucks still survive. The beam pumping engine was worked by water from the stream. Just above it, two miners' cottages have been restored to show the home life of the miner. The first shows an interior of the 1740s. There is an excellent short tape recounting the 18th century miner's living conditions, while the dire shortage of light imposed by the Window Tax is vividly demonstrated. The second interior shows the considerable easing of the miner's living conditions towards the end of the 19th century.

At the end of the trail is the Old Bay Mine (named curiously after the convict settlement in Botany Bay), where William Symington, the engineer who was born in Leadhills and spent much of his life working at Wanlockhead, erected his first atmospheric pumping engine.

WICK (H)

Wick Heritage Museum

20 Bank Row, Wick, Caithness
KW1 5EY   (0955) 3268
Closed October to May, otherwise closed Sundays. ⬛
♿ S: inaccessible to wheelchairs; difficult stairs for disabled/infirm. ⛟ & ⛟ welcome but must book in advance.

Early on in your visit to this museum you are led to the gallery on the first floor. The display here is dominated by photographs of the Johnston family, which are among the greatest treasures of the Centre. William Johnston was a plumber who came to Wick in 1828 to cover the roof of the parish kirk with lead. His son Alexander, born in 1839, was no doubt also apprenticed to the plumber's trade, but he turned instead to photography and opened a studio in Wick in 1861. By the end, three generations of the family had worked as photographers at Wick, producing over 100,000 negatives, which were given to the Wick Heritage Society in 1978.

These photographs form a rare and precious archive, recording almost every aspect of life in Wick and the surrounding district – the fishing industry with the sailing boats and fisher girls, haymaking and other rural activities, the railway, the early motor cars, the streets and shops, the people. They range over Caithness as far as John o' Groats and Thurso. Many of them are at the same time beautiful early examples of the art. In another room of the museum is the photographic equipment used by the Johnstons, including an enlarger and a big studio camera mounted on a trolley.

The Johnston collection is supplemented by albums of mainly later photographs, which the visitor is invited to consult at the table provided, recording everything from the Wick Herring Queen to a giant squid found on Ackergill beach.

Beyond the gallery is a series of 'period rooms', one with a box bed,

Alexander Johnston's camera and enlarger

Pewter communion cup, 1773

another with an ornate iron bedstead, and a kitchen and parlour. The parlour has a bible in large print given by a man to his son in 1858 lying open on the table, with a portable gramophone of the 1920s close by and ornaments ranging from High Victorian to Art Nouveau round the fireplace. It is not impossible for these things to have been together, but it raises the question what period is intended, and some labelling might be helpful.

If we have reservations about the merits of the period rooms, they are in any case by no means unique to the Wick museum and therefore of secondary interest to the tourist coming from outside. On the other hand, there can be no complaint about the authenticity, or the explanations, of what is on show elsewhere. The route leads past the lantern of the old Noss Head lighthouse of 1849 (we see its machinery underneath later on), and then a reconstruction shows how the herring were hung on racks or 'tenters' before being put in kilns to be cured. (The collection is housed mainly in an old curing barn for herrings and the yard outside.)

Next is a large area devoted to the sea and fishing, with a breeches buoy slung right across it. We find here models of boats; a herring gutting machine; a loud hailer; a binnacle of 1910; a harpoon gun; storm signals; a rocket gun; and stencil plates for the herring barrels. There is also a VHF transmitter from the BBC and the transmitter from the GPO radio station of Wick, used from 1910 to signal to home and Atlantic fleets (it was the last in a chain of transmitters up the British coast). Odd corners are filled up with ropes, lines, nets and creels.

From here we look down on a tableau of the harbour with boats preparing to go out. Along a side wall is a very good display on a noticeboard, headed 'Some Facts', which illustrates the harsh reality of life in Wick in the 19th century. For example, during the 1861 season there were 5,000 fishermen, 3,000 gutters, 600 coopers and 94 fish-curing firms. In 1911 there were 169 sailing boats and 22 steam boats. The population and the activity de-

The harbour scene

clined when the economics of the industry began to demand larger boats than the harbour could hold. By 1940 there were no large motor boats left there.

Downstairs there is an outstanding reconstruction of a cooper's shed, coopering being of course one of the essential ancillaries of the fishing industry, and nearby is a good illustrated account of how the barrels were made.

More displays are in preparation, some of them in the old fish curing yard outside.

At the time of writing the guide book was out of print, but a detailed account of a feud between rival factions in the town in 1850, 'The War of the Orange', begins with an excellent view of what the town was like in its heyday at the height of the fishing season in August.

Isle of Lewis (O)
ARNOL

Arnol Blackhouse

Arnol, Isle of Lewis (031) 244 3101
Closed Sundays.
: all on one level, but narrow doors.
 & arrange in advance by telephone: (031) 244 3101/3087.

The Arnol blackhouse stands apart from comparable houses that can be seen elsewhere. For one thing, under the strict definition of a blackhouse as one of the original houses with no chimney to allow the smoke from the fire to escape, it may now actually be unique. Besides this, by being in´the care of the Scottish Development Department, it has the advantage of adequate resources, but it also acquires somehow an official standing, like Edinburgh Castle or Skara Brae, as well as an authoritative and well-produced booklet, which looks at the whole history of blackhouses on Lewis and the social and economic pattern of crofting life.

The house is no. 42 in the village of Arnol, where some of the old black-houses, now mostly without their straw thatched roofs, survive side by side with more recent houses made of concrete blocks. The outside is disting-

The kitchen, with kettle hanging over the central hearth

uished by a roof with rounded ends, the thatch held down by ropes attached to stones, while the walls project well beyond it all round and are squared off at the corners. Light is provided by one small window with fixed panes, which is in the bedroom, and some six small rectangular rooflights. The smoke from the peat fire, which burned in the middle of the stone floor, was left to

View of the croft from the back

The barn roof

find its way through the thatch, which gradually decomposed to form potash that would be used for fertilising the fields when the thatch was renewed.

The house and byre are under the same long roof, with the barn running behind them and sharing the back wall. The main entrance and the doorway to the barn lie opposite each other. A blocked-up opening in line with them, in the far wall of the barn, ensured the through draught that was needed for winnowing.

Most of these blackhouses are not in fact as old as they appear. No. 42 Arnol dates from about 1875. And suddenly, at the sight of a photograph of people living in one of these Lewis black-houses in 1934, I am stopped short. Here, in a house and in a mode of living that seems to be so far away in time, is a man wearing the kind of cap and 'plus fours' I used to see my uncle in Edinburgh wearing at that time, and smoking his kind of pipe. Immediately I have a sense of intruding into these people's lives, the same sense that overtakes me in looking through the personal belongings of the Toward family in the Glasgow tenement house, now with the National Trust for Scotland. There is something sad, too, in the lino and wallpaper covering the kind of floor and walls that strike the town-dweller as primitive, as though the inhabitants were doing their best to keep up with urban fashions. We meet this again in the comparable houses on **Skye**, whereas **Kirbuster** in Orkney has lost whatever dressing the walls had and no doubt gives a more primitive impression than it did when it was last inhabited.

Something of my own sense of intrusion comes out in the 'Personal Impression' given by Alexander Fenton in his preface to the booklet. But the custodian who welcomes you to the house sees it from an altogether different perspective. She grew up in the house as a girl, and recorded her experiences at the time: 'During the winter', she wrote, 'many neighbours come in each night ... During the summer many tourists come ... asking to see the three legged pot hanging over the fire.'

Orkney (O)
CORRIGALL and KIRBUSTER

Orkney Farm & Folk Museum

Corrigall, Harray, Orkney
KW17 2HZ   (0856) 77411
and
Kirbuster, Birsay, Orkney
KW17 2LW   (0856) 72268
Closed November to February.
⬛ joint admission; ◨ to OAPs and children.
♿ & 🚻 must book in advance.

These are two crofts lying about seven miles apart in open countryside, Kirbuster having been gifted only recently. Both are administered from **Tankerness House** in Kirkwall, and admission is by a common entrance ticket. It might be thought that there would be too much of an overlap between the two locations, but they are being made to complement one another, showing two different aspects of Orkney life.

In some ways Kirbuster, which is furthest afield, is the more fascinating. Lying close to a small loch, looking across the gently rolling land that is characteristic of Orkney towards the Hills of Miffia to the south, it was in its day one of the more substantial farm-houses of its kind.

The visitor enters through a room now used for showing the construction and history of the farmhouse, which then leads into the oldest part of the building, the heart of the museum and the prime reason for acquiring the croft. This part is the last surviving example of the old 'firehooses', as they were called. Here were the living quarters for the family and for some of the animals. The date 1723 on an old re-used lintel may be the date of this building, but a parish record of 1595 already refers to a firehoose on this site.

It looks more primitive than it does in the old photographs, now that the

Corrigall: the living room or 'in-bye'

lime plaster and wallpaper is stripped off. But this is what the Orkney 'fire-hooses' looked like until the early 19th century. And when you go there, you are likely to find a peat fire burning, an essential ingredient in what it felt like, and smelt like, too. The fire is located towards the middle of the space, built up against a low stone wall, with a kettle hanging from a beam above (colour plate 3). Offset by several feet is the 'lum', a short, square wooden chimney to draw off the smoke, with an outrigger board above, which is moved round on a pole to hold off the prevailing wind.

A particular feature of Orkney houses was the roof made of Orkney stone flags, used like slates as they were plentiful and split readily into even layers. On the inside of the roof these were left uncovered. A good deal

Kirbuster: outbuildings with circular kiln

Corrigall: passageway between the living quarters (left) and the barn and byre

Kirbuster: hearth and low wall separating the 'in-bye' and 'oot-bye'

of the smoke from the fire finds its way out eventually, and used to pass across meat and fish hung in the roof space for smoking. Behind the fire was the family's living area, known as the 'in-bye', while the work ox, the pig and poultry were brought in to the other side of the fire-back, the 'oot-bye'. The bed, called a 'neuk bed', predecessor of the box bed, is an alcove in the wall with the ubiquitous Orkney stone flags on either side of the access to protect the sleepers from the draught.

Kirbuster farm was only taken over in 1986, and although it was still lived in until 1961, a great deal of restoration work remains to be done. Apart from later additions to the buildings, there is a round kiln typical of Orkney, which is very beautiful to look at inside, and – a vivid reminder of the self-sufficiency that was required of these crofts – a diminutive smithy behind the pig sty. Visitors are likely to find a pig as well as other animals in residence when they come, and the caretaker is herself a mine of first-hand information about the way of life on these crofts.

An unusually long out-building houses a display of farm implements, including a pit saw used to cut the larger pieces of driftwood that came to hand, and two wooden rollers made from ships' masts.

What the visitor sees at Corrigall is a later development from around the middle of the 19th century. The living quarters with the kiln at one end and the single building serving as byre and barn were built parallel to each other with a flagged passageway six feet wide in between. The byre preserves its flagged floor and the stone stalls for cattle. The 'in-bye' now has a regular hearth and is separated from the 'oot-bye', with another room for box beds beyond. On the far side of the oot-bye was the byre, the cattle coming in through the same door as the family. This was later converted for use as the best parlour or to sleep a farm servant, and is now used for museum display, including an 18th century loom. The nearby barn has a kiln of the circular type not uncommon in Orkney.

The problem of giving the visitor information unobtrusively is effectively solved in both crofts. Information 'bats' ares provided to hold in the hand, elegantly hand-written with simple drawings to help identify objects, and the objects are introduced in an order that makes an understanding of their functions in the life of the croft easy to follow: for instance things used in brewing, the 'platting tub' in which a pig was scalded after it was killed to remove the bristles, or the 'klibber', a wooden pack saddle with straw paniers for carrying peat on the horse.

KIRKWALL

Tankerness House Museum

Broad Street, Kirkwall, Orkney
KW15 1DH   (0856) 3191
Closed Sundays October to April.
⬛ but ◼ to OAPs and children.
&: first floor inaccessible to
wheelchairs.
🚹 & 🚻 welcome, preferably book
in advance

This building is a fine 16th century
town house standing in its own courtyard opposite St Magnus Cathedral,
with an ornamental garden behind. It
was considerably altered and enlarged
in the early part of the 18th century,
and was lived in by the Baikies, a
distinguished Orkney family. It was
fully restored in 1968.

The museum, which is administered
by Orkney Islands Council, is the
headquarters of the historical
museums in Orkney, since **Corrigall**
and **Kirbuster** are branch museums,
and **Stromness Museum**, although
run by an independent trust, also relies
on the services of the curator in Kirkwall.

In the allocation of different subjects
Tankerness House took on responsibility for Orkney archaeology. The
most recently arranged display is on
the ground floor, opened in 1985. Called 'The First Settlers', it aims to tell
the story of the Neolithic and Bronze
Ages in Orkney, that is the story of the
settlers from 5,000 years ago. The way
it is told is unusual; the plan of the
exhibition is intelligently thought out
and the presentation is clear, although
in places visually unattractive. Visitors
are appealed to directly to think for
themselves what it was like being the
first people to settle on the island: what
could be found to eat, or for shelter, or
for making dwellings or clothes. You
are made to realise for example what
the form of the buildings and their
furnishings depended upon: the plentiful supply of Orkney flag stones, with

A living room as used by the Baikie family in the 1820s

their straight grain that allowed them
to be split like slate into large flat slabs,
and the fact that the environment was
hostile to trees, so that most of the
timber had to be found in the form of
driftwood. At the same time the point
is made that what has survived to us
from these peoples is only what was
durable enough to survive: bone, stone,
metal and little else. The language is
deliberately direct, for instance: 'The
sea was an open highway. It brought
driftwood and dead whales . . . ' or
'You need clothes. How are you going
to make them? Use the hide and sinew
from the animals you have killed.'

To support this narrative, as much
sense as possible is made of the objects
on show, for instance by showing the
axe and mace heads with handles, or by
showing Unstan pottery on a reconstruction of a stone dresser from Skara
Brae.

The section on ritual – the area
about which we want to know most, but
know least – is very good. Among the
artefacts is the Neolithic stone from
Westray with its strangely beautiful
design of spirals, which is perhaps the
finest of its kind found in the UK.
There is also an account of the cham-
bered tomb, the 'Tomb of the Eagles',

excavated at Isbister. This is accompanied by an impressive array of skulls
and bones set out to give an impression
of the remains of over 300 early settlers
that were found there. And finally,
there is a display showing the ancient
monuments that are to be seen in
Orkney.

The exhibition is memorable not
only for its approach to presenting the

16th century gateway to Tankerness House

rather intractable facts of archaeology to a wide public, but also because it was made the occasion for the return to Orkney on loan of three of the objects discovered there from the **National Museums of Scotland** where they had hitherto been housed.

Upstairs – and the stairwell itself is a pretty curve with the curved stair-rail continuing on the landing – are two rooms that are seen somewhat as the Baikie family had them in the 1820s. (The white walls seem surprising but may well have been a preference in Orkney at this time.) There are more archaeological finds in the displays on this floor including a group of Pictish and Norse combs made from bone and often decorated. The absence of some of the most dramatic finds is a keen disappointment, because it tends to be the most valuable – and therefore the most finely wrought – of the works of craftsmanship that we must go to Edinburgh to see. The Scoto-Viking Skaill hoard, found at Skaill in 1858, included not only silver brooches and armlets from some time after 950 AD but coins that were struck in Baghdad. It is represented here only by black and white photographs. So is the Westness brooch, a silver Celtic brooch of the 8th century inset with gold panels, amber studs and red glass, although this was found as recently as 1963. [The brooch was among the objects that were lent to Tankerness House for six months in 1989. Ed.]

Among displays of later objects are an extremely small printing press of 1821, the first to be used in Orkney; the bell from the parish church of Birsay cast in 1605; types of straw work produced in Orkney (straw was much used, for instance in the making of chairs, but the range extends to remarkably delicate plaiting in straw hats); an interesting group of crusie lamps; and some beautiful communion cups and flagons, one of them dated 1814. The curious and evidently tumultuous Kirkwall ball game, or 'ba' game', which has been played around Christmas time between the two parts of the town, the 'uppies' and the 'doonies', since the early years of last century, is recorded in photographs.

STROMNESS

Pier Arts Centre

Victoria Street, Stromness, Orkney
KW16 3AA   (0856) 850209
Closed Mondays; also closed
Sundays September to May. **F**
&: first floor accessible only by
narrow stairs.
♿ & ♿ welcome but must book in
advance.

One of the most delightful surprises the museum world has to offer the unsuspecting visitor is to turn down a narrow passage off the paved main street of Stromness and into the building beyond, with an abstract sculpture by Barbara Hepworth standing on the quayside outside it. In the 1830s the building used to house the recruiting agent for the Hudson's Bay Company (see the notes on **Stromness Museum**). The interior was reconstructed as an arts centre, mainly to house the art collection which Margaret Gardiner of London gave to Orkney.

The gallery was opened in 1979, and the unusual circumstances that brought it about are charmingly recounted by Margaret Gardiner herself in 'The Pier Gallery: the first ten years', published by the Centre in 1988. Margaret Gardiner had brought the works together in her London house, some of them acquired during the 1920s and '30s but mostly soon after the war. She got to know Orkney at the end of the 1950s, and later decided to devote herself to establishing a permanent home there for her collection (although she finds the word 'collecting' inappropriate to describe what she did).

The focus of the collection is a group of works by Ben Nicholson and Barbara Hepworth. The first one she bought was the lively and unexpected 'Fireworks', painted by Ben Nicholson in 1929, and its combination of serious

Upstairs galleries, looking across the stairwell

The courtyard, with Barbara Hepworth's
Curved form (Trevalgan) *of 1956*

abstract art and the fun of fireworks seems to symbolise the sense of delight with which Margaret Gardiner responded to the things she bought. The great majority of the paintings and sculptures are abstract. Yet at this distance in time from when they were made, mostly between the mid-1940s and early 1960s, partly because of their environment here, they seem to have lost much of their doctrinaire severity. Some indeed, like those of Peter Lanyon and Eduardo Paolozzi, never had this element of purism or puritanism. But even Barbara Hepworth's 'Oval Sculpture' of 1943, with its plain rectangular perspex case and rectilinear pedestal, is so much at home here that it becomes a gentle, almost human presence.

It is in fact this friendliness, and the impression that the things are at home here, that make the experience of the visit. The reconstruction of the interior was designed with the collection in view, and took fully into account the nature of the works it contained. The floors are covered with dun-coloured cord carpet, and the walls and ceilings are white, with only the ventilators and spotlights in the ceiling painted black in contrast. Some of the walls upstairs are only three feet high where the slope of the roof begins. The windows here – and the paintings on the wall too – are correspondingly low down, and except for an occasional skylight the main daylight comes from these low windows. Other walls are the old room-divisions which have been cut away to allow a sense of the complete space.

The head of the stair is opposite a full-length window that looks out onto the pier and boats, with the Hepworth sculpture in the courtyard immediately below and the low Orcadian hills beyond. Beside the window are one of the most serene of Ben Nicholson's paintings and a bizarre plaster relief by Eduardo Paolozzi. Perhaps it is not by accident that the shapes of the boats outside the window linger in the mind as you look at the paintings and sculptures in the rooms. Most of these works come from another community with a strong sense of the sea, at St Ives in Cornwall.

The creation of the Centre might have been no more than a whim that came to nothing, and many eyebrows were raised at the time at the apparent eccentricity of plonking down the products of a very sophisticated group of artists from the far south of England among the people of Stromness, most of whom could never have seen anything like them. The fact that this did not happen, that the Pier Arts Centre has come to be not only a place of pilgrimage for tourists but a centre of activity for the people of Orkney, is partly due to the decision to extend its use not only for temporary exhibitions but for all kinds of other arts activities as well. The first and only curator till now has seen to it that the necessary liveliness and energy are maintained. A long, low gallery downstairs is reserved for temporary exhibitions, and it is also the venue for lectures and other events. The exhibitions are of contemporary art, often but by no means always by Orcadians.

Stromness Museum

52 Alfred Street, Stromness, Orkney
(0856) 850025
Closed Sundays. ▣
&: wheelchair access to ground floor only.
🎒 & ♟ welcome, preferably book in advance.

The museum is administered by the Orkney Natural History Society, and this gives the clue to its origins and original purpose. The society was founded in 1837, with the object of promoting natural science and collecting specimens of natural history and antiquities in Orkney. One of the early members was the geologist Hugh Miller, and among the fossils in the museum is his so-called petrified nail, or more properly the *Homosteus milleri*, which he found in 1843 and gave to the museum. The building itself was put up in 1858 to house the museum on the upper floor and the Stromness Town Hall below. In 1929 it was taken over entirely by the museum.

Scuttled German battleship SMS 'Bayern'
raised in 1934 by Metal Industries Ltd

Boat model and seafaring artefacts

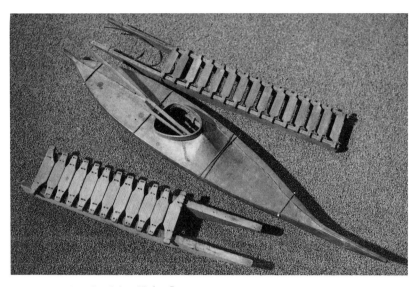

Sledges and Eskimo kayak from Hudson Bay

The first floor is devoted to the natural history of Orkney. This is perhaps more valuable to the tourist than in many places, for even a towns-man cannot spend long on the island without becoming curious about its wildlife, the birds in particular: the fulmars, puffins and cormorants, and the osprey and the golden eagle are both occasional visitors. There is no reason to regret that the exhibits are shown in old fashioned showcases. They are clearly seen, with brief but adequate descriptions. Among other examples of wildlife is a very good collection of crustacea, showing some of the range and variety of these crea-tures. There are also specimens of the rocks found on the islands, and a group of fossil fish, a number of them found in the Stromness flagstones. (Perhaps the three-foot-long slob trout caught in Stenness Loch in 1889 should count as a curiosity rather than a natural history specimen.)

In the present distribution between Orkney museums, Stromness has given up archaeology to **Tankerness House** in **Kirkwall**, has retained its responsibility for natural history, and has taken on the history of the Orca-dian connection with the sea because Stromness has always been the main Orcadian focus for this. There are

Herring boats in Stromness harbour

models of boats, including the Orkney version of the yole. There are relics salvaged from wrecks, like the 'Svecia' of 1740 which was being dredged from 1975. There is the terrible history of Eliza Fraser (the subject of one of the annual temporary exhibitions here), who was ship-wrecked on the Great Barrier Reef to see her husband the ship's captain murdered whilst she herself was enslaved by the Aborigines until her rescue in 1836. A sea-chest, with nicely inlaid floral decorations inside the lid instead of the more usual naive painting of a ship at sea, has the effect of making mutiny at sea suddenly vivid. It belonged to Captain John Smith of Cockleha' in Tanker-ness. Trading in the Chinese seas with crews of Malays and Lascars, he always slept with a brace of loaded pistols beside his bed, but was killed in the end by mutineers in 1853.

Orkney had particularly close links with the Hudson's Bay Company. Stromness, due east of Hudson Bay, was the first landfall for the company's ships. Up to the end of the last century the company maintained a staff there, and at the south end of the town there is a gun that was fired to announce the arrival of Hudson's Bay Company ships. Many Orcadians served with the company, and indeed in the latter 18th century they represented over three-quarters of the company's complete staff. Among the souvenirs brought back is a delicate Eskimo carving in bone of a sleigh with its team of dogs, one of the earliest gifts to the museum.

Another display concerns Arctic ex-plorers. One of them, Sir John Frank-lin (1786–1847), sought a passage to the Pacific via the Arctic – the 'North West passage' that had been sought for so long – but his ship disappeared after leaving via Stromness for the Arctic in 1846. It was an Orkneyman and one of the earliest members of the Natural History Society, Dr John Rae (1813–93), a distinguished explorer for the Hudson's Bay Company, who led the expedition that finally, eight years later, discovered what had happened to Franklin.

Travelling along the south side of the Orkney mainland, round Scapa Flow, the visitor is reminded, by the forlorn turrets that stick out of the water, of the scuppering of the German fleet there in 1918. These are in fact ships sunk by the British in an attempt to block submarine attack. The museum gives an account of the Ger-man scuppering and of subsequent sal-vage operations, with photographs and documents, and with relics saved from the wrecks.

Not to be overlooked are the museum's publications, which repre-sent continuing research and are gra-dually covering much of Orkney's his-tory, ranging from modest catalogues of their temporary exhibitions to an outstanding if harrowing account of the ice-bound whalers. And this last also gives a full account of the Natural History Society and its museum.

Shetland (O)
LERWICK

Shetland Museum

Lower Hillhead, Lerwick, Shetland
ZE1 OEL   (0595) 5057
Closed Sundays. ▣
&: access by staircase only.

The building dates from 1966, and marks the establishment of Shetland Museum and its collections on a regular basis under the aegis of the Shetland Islands Council. The library is on the ground floor and the museum occupies the whole of the top floor, which is a not inconsiderable area. A curiosity of the building is that, although presumably purpose built to house the museum, the outside walls are all window, so that the display area is reduced and reflections are unnecessarily troublesome.

Displays take a fairly conventional form in showcases, but the objects are clearly set out with adequate and not excessive descriptions in typewritten labels. Arrangement by theme for each showcase makes it possible to relate isolated objects, and here and there simple but imaginative help is given to visualising the way things were used, as for example the 'clam', the mould used for making horn spoons. Again, one of the early trough querns is shown with a grinding stone in it and some corn that has been ground into grain, and later methods of grinding corn are shown beside it.

It is not difficult to realise how much of the life and history of Shetland is bound up with the sea, and the museum illuminates this. One favoured form of boat, the yole, was light and fast. (The name, presumably the same as yawl, is of Norse derivation.) Models are here, and the museum also has a seaworthy yole in its collection. Whalers did not set out from Shetland, nor were they built on the island, but Lerwick was a natural port of call and Shetlanders were frequently taken on as crew. A display on whaling shows the kinds of whale, the harpoons, the flensing knives and other tools. It also gives some insight, in the space available, into the terrible hardships of the whaling men. In

Monk's stone from Papil, Burra Isle

another case is the 'ditty box' containing the personal mementoes and souvenirs of John Hutchison. He was one of the survivors from the whaler 'Diana' when it was trapped in the ice in the winter of 1866/7 and many of the crew died of scurvy or starvation.

We quickly learn, too, that the difficulty of growing trees in the islands made wood extremely scarce, and much of the wood used was driftwood washed up on the shore. Driftwood implies wrecks, a pressing reminder of the darker side of the sea. Two of the historic wrecks off the Shetland coast are commemorated here, the 'De Liefde' of 1711, which was being salvaged from 1965, and the still older wreck of the 'Kennermerland' of 1664. Another case contains 'sea brucks', objects brought to the surface while dredging for scallops. And there are beautiful coins salvaged from wrecks. Spanish reals, silver and gold ducats and other 17th century coins.

There are good cases of local rocks and minerals, some of them polished, including semi-precious stones like agate, jasper, quartz, amethyst, and samples of iron, lead, copper and zinc ores. Probably of less interest to the tourist is a gallery reserved for temporary exhibitions, mainly of the work of local artists and craftsmen. (It is also used for lectures, slide shows and as a schoolroom.)

Among farm implements that are of more than local interest are the Norwegian 'trauch' (a serving dish for

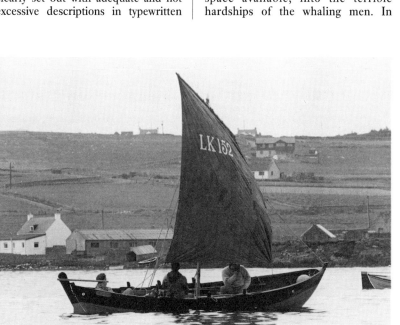

Restored 'yoal' fishing boat used in museum events

food), saddles and panniers for the Shetland ponies, the gear for cutting and gathering peat, and a large one-stilted (i.e. single-handled) plough of 1864. Other Victoriana include the first telephone installed in Shetland in 1883 and one of the first typewriters, also of 1883, before the keyboard was standardised.

A prehistoric 'ard' plough preserved in the peat and the early Christian 'Monks stone' from Papil, Burra Isle, are among the plentiful survivals from earlier phases of our civilisation, which are among the more distinctive features of Shetland. These include in particular the Pictish 'brochs' (ancient strongholds). Many of the artefacts recovered from the brochs can be seen in the museum, for instance from the Clickimin broch in Lerwick itself and from the great *Jarlshof* settlement in the south. For the ordinary visitor looking at archaeological finds, the temperature rises in front of things like the Gulberwick brooch, a Norse product in solid silver of the 10th century. Its crisp ornamentation represents a love of craftsmanship to which most of us respond more readily than to an axehead. But here disappointment awaits, for many of the most interesting finds from Shetland are kept in the **National Museums** in **Edinburgh**, whilst the visitor to Lerwick can see only casts.

Frustration is greatest over the famous St Ninian's Treasure. St Ninian's Isle lies to the south of Lerwick, approached by a narrow causeway of sand. Up on the hill overlooking the mainland there had been a chapel, later built over by a medieval church. The chapel was discovered in the 1950s, and excavation brought to light a marvellous hoard of 28 silver bowls, brooches and other things (colour plate 10) which had been hidden away in a box under the floor of the chapel at some time around 800 AD. The treasure was discovered in the 1950s, at a time when Shetland had no museum that could look after it adequately, and it has since been kept in Edinburgh. All we can see in the Lerwick museum is a set of copies, displayed with all the care due to original artefacts, and an illustrated booklet.

Isle of Skye (H)
ARMADALE

The Clan Donald Centre (Museum of the Isles)

Armadale, Ardvasar, Sleat, Isle of Skye IV45 8RS   (04714) 305/227
Closed November to Easter. 🅵 🖳 🅿
♿ **W**: wheelchairs available.
👥 & 👫 welcome, advisable to book in advance so that staff can help with preparation and visit itself.

The Centre is worth a visit for anyone interested in learning about the earlier history of Scotland. Whether it should be included at present among museums is arguable. It has been included here not so much on the strength of the existing collection, for this is small and a proportion of it is on loan, but more for the purpose the Centre aims to serve and its intentions for the future. It is certainly the most ambitious and the best appointed among the several clan museums and clan centres.

The museum is housed in the former 'mansion house' part of Armadale Castle. Part of the Castle was built by Gillespie Graham in 1815, while the centre part was rebuilt by David Bryce in 1858 after a fire, and was lived in by the Macdonald family until 1925. It then lay empty, and has now been made safe, with one end made into a 'sculptured ruin'. The whole estate, including woodlands and extensive hill farms and crofts, was bought by the Clan Donald Lands Trust a year after its formation in 1972. The Centre has received substantial support from members of the clan, especially the branches that are now in America. The whole complex has been extensively rebuilt and enlarged, and it now comprises living accommodation, craft shop and restaurant, a nature trail supported by a Countryside Ranger service, as well as the museum, library and archive, whose remit covers the history of Gaeldom and the Clan Donald in particular.

An outstanding feature of the museum is an audio-visual programme. Called 'The Sea Kingdom', it lasts for 18 minutes, reviewing the history of the islands from the Pictish stone circles up to the time of the Highland clearances. The audience is given a lively and unusually vivid insight into the rich and sophisticated culture of the Gaels, which flourished for a period of four centuries under the Lordship of the Isles, and was finally submerged in the clash with the wholly alien and unsympathetic Anglo-Norman society during the medieval era.

A major part of the museum area is at present taken up with a highly professional and well mounted display of texts, dramatised in places by being lit behind cut-out figures of clansmen. To the emotive accompaniment of the

Armadale Castle, with later buildings now part of the museum

sound of the sea, pipes, clarsach (harp) and song, these take the visitor through the extent and administration of the Lordship of the Isles; a genealogy of the clan; the achievements of the Gaelic poets, musicians, physicians, lawyers and craftsmen; and the eventual decline of the culture. What we are seeing, however, are basically only texts, although elegantly and imaginatively presented, and they are also available in a booklet, 'The Headship of the Gael'.

The small collection is displayed in showcases in the last room to be visited. Curiously, the same degree of sophistication that is apparent in the presentation of the texts and in the audio-visual programme does not survive in the museum cases. [These are to be rearranged and upgraded in 1990. Ed.] But the exhibits include some very touching and occasionally splendid objects, a good many of them on loan from the descendants of the men with whom they and their accompanying legends are associated.

Here are the 'fairy pipes of Moidart'. They are inscribed 'Chanter, mouth-

Duelling pistols, c.1770–80 (on loan from the Glengarry)

piece and part of drone of Kinlochmoidart pipes played at Bannockburn (1314)', and the bag is covered with the ancient Clanranald tartan (ill. on cover). Duelling pistols from the 1770s, lent by the present Glengarry, belonged to his ancestor Alasdair Ranaldson Macdonell, well known through his portrait by Raeburn in the **National Gallery of Scotland**; he is believed to have used them in his duel with Lieutenant McLeod of the 42nd Regiment. Here, too, are sets of ornamented highland dirks made in the 19th century for use by the family of Lord Macdonald.

KILMUIR

Skye Museum of Island Life

Kilmuir, Portree, Isle of Skye
(047052) 279
Closed November to Easter, otherwise closed Sundays. ⓈⓅ
♿ S: rough going for wheelchairs.

The buildings that make up this museum lie up on a hillside near the northern end of Skye, and the visitor approaches them from below. To the west the land falls away again, leaving an open view across the sea towards the Western Isles. The general aspect of the place suggests that what we are seeing is the buildings of a complete crofting community as it was, rather similar to **Auchindrain** near Inveraray, and to a large extent this is true.

The principal building is a croft house of unusual size. This was built in the mid-19th century, with one of the two main rooms intended to accommodate the children of a family of Victorian proportions. It was inhabited continuously up to 1960, and was in fact chosen as the cottage for the late George VI and HRH Queen Elizabeth the Queen Mother to visit when they went to Skye as Duke and Duchess of York in 1933. There are then two other buildings in line with the croft house. One that is now called the Weaver's Cottage almost abuts it, and nearby down the hill, built so that the roof thatch is almost level with the ground at one end, is a building that was known as the 'Ceilidh House' (the ceilidh – pronounced 'cailey' – being a social gathering).

Near to these buildings, which belong to the old community or clachan, are two others – a Barn and a Smithy. These, however, have been built from new in the space of the last few years. The nature of their construction, with cobbled floor, stone walls and thatching held down against the wind by stones attached to wires, follows faith-

19th century Highland dirks (on loan from Lord MacDonald of the Isles)

General view with part of the croft house on the left

fully the traditional pattern. One of the great strengths of the folk museum movement in Scotland, which we find again at the **Highland Folk Museum, Kingussie**, is its success in keeping alive – and sometimes recovering – the old building skills. (In the case of thatching this is obviously a necessity.)

The apparatus of the Smithy, to judge for instance by the smithy at **Auchindrain**, is authentic, and a sign at the wall indicates that it is the shop of Donald McMillan, native of Inverness-shire. As a reconstruction it deserves nothing but praise, but the name it is given, 'the old smithy', gives the misleading impression that a smithy stood in this place in the original disposition of the buildings, and that a barn was built near to it. Unfortunately this tends to undermine the reliability of the museum. What the visitor requires is to be able to visualise what the life of the crofter was like in this place, and it is essential to know how much of what we see is authentic and how much is not.

The Barn houses a collection of the farm implements that were once in use, including comparatively familiar things like the quern stones used for grinding grain, as well as a 'wrack sickle', 'swingle tree' and 'thrawcrook'. Their uses are explained in labels.

The interiors of the original three houses are, of course, not furnished as they were. The living room of the croft house is furnished convincingly as it might have been, including a fireside seat made out of an old herring barrel. On the dresser is a surprising collection of mugs celebrating royal occasions from Queen Victoria's Jubilee of 1897 onwards. A peat fire burns in the grate – not infrequently needed for its warmth, even in the summer season, and a source of fascination to foreign visitors. An inner room is partitioned off with the box bed and clothes chest.

The back room where the children slept is used partly for a display of books about the islands and partly for a small museum collection. Some of this seems to be of a different vintage from the display of implements in the barn, both in its more primitive presentation and in the impression of less rigorous research, but it contains much of interest. There is a pewter communion cup from the old thatched church at

Trumpan above Dunvegan; a pulpit bible from the ruined church on the now uninhabited island of Rona, between Skye and the mainland (in English because Gaelic was at that time proscribed); a sample bottle of illicit whisky taken from a house in Breakish in 1913, with a label attached signed by the excise man and the crofter (who was not convicted). We are also reminded that this was Flora Macdonald country by an alabaster egg cup that reputedly was once hers, and an iron pot reputedly used by her to prepare a meal for the Bonnie Prince.

The interior of the Weaver's House is dominated by a large hand-loom from the late 19th century. Its roof is a clear example of the traditional method of thatching, with wooden rafters and purlins carrying a layer of turf underneath the reeds. The Ceilidh House was in fact lived in by the tailor, no doubt one who was socially inclined. It is now used for an exhibition of documents, particularly old photographs of life on the islands.

A booklet with good illustrations and very brief notes on the buildings has recently been produced by the founder and present curator. Opened as a museum in 1965, Kilmuir is still being developed, and by September 1988 two more buildings were in the process of being completed.

In the kitchen of the croft house

Museums in Scotland

The list below is sub-divided into regions, arranged alphabetically, which correspond to the maps pp. 112–116. Museums shown in **bold** are described fully in the main text of this volume.

Please note that in the case of branch museums listed below, the telephone number for enquiries may be in a different building, or even a different town.

BORDERS REGION

BROUGHTON

John Buchan Heritage Centre
Broughton, Biggar ML12 6HQ
(0899) 21050

Dedicated to John Buchan, author, lawyer, soldier, poet and Governor General of Canada.

COLDSTREAM

Coldstream Museum
Market Square, Coldstream,
Berwickshire TD12   (0890) 2630

On the site of the original Coldstream Guards headquarters; displays on the regiment's history, and agricultural items.

The Homestead Museum
The Hirsel, Coldstream, Berwickshire
(0890) 2834

In a Victorian stable block; displays on the Home family, the estate, its archaeology and natural history.

DUNS

Jim Clark Memorial Room
44 Newton Street, Duns,
Berwickshire TD11   (0361) 82600

Trophies won by the motor racing champion, a native of Duns.

EYEMOUTH

Eyemouth Museum

HAWICK

Hawick Museum & The Scott Gallery

JEDBURGH

Castle Jail
Castlegate, Jedburgh TD8 6QD
(0835) 63254

A Howard reform prison of 1823; exhibits relating to 19th century prison life.

Mary Queen of Scots House
Queen Street, Jedburgh TD8 6EN
(0835) 63331

A fine 16th century bastel house; exhibits concern the Queen and her visit to Jedburgh.

KELSO

Kelso Museum
Turret House, Abbey Court, Kelso
TD5 7JA   (0573) 25470

In a 17th century house; history of Kelso district, especially its trades.

MELROSE

Melrose Abbey
Melrose, Roxburghshire
(031) 244 3101 or 3087

The Commendator's house contains exhibits on the abbey's history and the Roman fort at Newstead.

PEEBLES

The Cornice
31 High Street, Peebles EH45 8AN
(0721) 20212

An ornamental plasterer's shop; explanations of how ornamental plaster is produced, with occasional demonstrations.

Tweeddale Museum & Picture Gallery
Chambers Institute, High Street,
Peebles EH45 8AJ   (0721) 20123

Small local museum with changing displays on the heritage of the area.

SELKIRK

Halliwell's House & Robson Gallery

WALKERBURN

Museum of Woollen Textiles
Tweedvale Mills, Walkerburn
EH43 6AH   (089 687) 281/283

A series of tableaux illustrating the history of the industry up to the present.

CENTRAL REGION

ALLOA

Alloa Museum
15 Mar Street, Alloa FK10 1HT
(0259) 722262

A small museum of mainly local interest.

BO'NESS

Bo'ness Heritage Trust

Kinneil Museum & Roman Fortlet
Duchess Anne Cottages, Kinneil
Estate, Bo'ness EH51 0PR
(0324) 24911 ext. 2202

The social and industrial history of Bo'ness illustrated by the history of the estate.

DOUNE

Doune Motor Museum

DUNBLANE

Dunblane Cathedral Museum

The Cross, Dunblane, Perthshire (0786) 822217

In the Dean's house of 1624; displays on the history of the town and cathedral.

FALKIRK

Falkirk Museum

15 Orchard Street, Falkirk FK1 1RF (0324) 24911 ext. 2202

Local history, including items from the Antonine Wall and medieval pottery from local kilns.

GRANGEMOUTH

Grangemouth Museum

Public Library, Bo'ness Road, Grangemouth FK3 8AG (0324) 24911 ext. 2202

Displays on the history of the town, centre of petroleum and chemical industries, and on the Forth & Clyde Canal.

STIRLING

The Argyll & Sutherland Highlanders Regimental Museum

The Castle, Stirling FK8 1EH (0786) 75165

Silver, colours, uniforms, medals and other militaria of the regiment, which was raised in 1794.

The Smith Art Gallery & Museum

DUMFRIES & GALLOWAY REGION

CLATTERINGSHAWS

Galloway Deer Museum

Clatteringshaws, New Galloway DG7 3SQ (06442) 285

A small museum on Galloway's red deer, wild goats and other local natural history.

CREETOWN

Creetown Gem-Rock Museum

DUMFRIES

Burns House

Burns Street, Dumfries DG1 2PS (0387) 55297

Burns' home for his last years; furnishings of the period and memorabilia.

Dumfries Museum & Camera Obscura

Dumfries Priory & Christian Heritage Museum

see under Strathclyde Region: *Largs Monastery Museum.*

Gracefield Arts Centre

28 Edinburgh Road, Dumfries DG1 1JQ (0387) 62084

A permanent collection of 19th and 20th century Scottish paintings; temporary art exhibitions.

Old Bridge House

Mill Road, Dumfries DG2 7BQ (0387) 56904

Built in the 17th century; 19th century period rooms include kitchen, nursery and dental laboratory.

Robert Burns Centre

Old Town Mill, Mill Road, Dumfries DG2 7BE (0387) 64808

Audio-visual programme and exhibition on Burns and his life in Dumfries.

GRETNA GREEN

Blacksmith's shop

Gretna Green, Dumfriesshire (0461) 38224

The old smithy with the marriage anvil, collection of coaches and illustrations of runaway couples.

HOLYWOOD

Ellisland Farm

Holywood Road, Dumfries DG2 0RW (0387) 74426

Farmhouse built by Robert Burns in 1785 containing Burns memorabilia; adjacent granary displaying agricultural implements.

KIRKCUDBRIGHT

Broughton House

12 High Street, Kirkcudbright DG6 4JX (0557) 30437

House, painting studio and Japanese garden of E.A. Hornel (1864–1933); pictures by him and the Glasgow School.

The Stewartry Museum

MOFFAT

Moffat Museum

The Neuk, Church Gate, Moffat DG10 9EG (0683) 20868

In a mid-19th century bakery; exhibits on the rise of Moffat as an Edwardian spa.

NEW ABBEY

Shambellie House Museum of Costume

NEWTON STEWART

The Museum
York Road, Newton Stewart,
Wigtownshire

Illustrates domestic and agricultural life of the area; Victorian nursery.

RUTHWELL

Savings Banks Museum

SANQUHAR

Sanquhar Museum
The Old Tolbooth, Sanquhar
DG4 6BL   (0387) 53374

Beautiful building of 1735 by William Adam, dominating the street; closed at present for reconstruction, revised plans for use under discussion at time of going to press.

STRANRAER

Stranraer Museum
The Old Town Hall, George Street,
Stranraer   (0776) 5088

Local history, including clockmaking in Wigtown and polar explorers John and James Ross.

WANLOCKHEAD

Museum of Scottish Lead Mining

WHITHORN

Whithorn Cathedral Priory Museum
Whithorn, Wigtownshire
(031) 244 3101/3087

Site of the first Scottish Christian church; contains some fine early Christian stones.

WIGTOWN

Wigtown Museum
Town Hall, Wigtown   (0776) 5088

Local history; special displays on the five Wigtown martyrs.

FIFE REGION

ANSTRUTHER

North Carr Light Vessel
The Harbour, Anstruther, Fife
(0334) 53722

Lightship which served in the North Sea 1938–75.

Scottish Fisheries Museum

BUCKHAVEN

Buckhaven Museum
College Street, Buckhaven, Fife
(0592) 260732

Small local history museum on Buckhaven's past importance as a fishing town.

BURNTISLAND

Burntisland Edwardian Fair
102 High Street, Burntisland
KY3 9AS

Newly recreated 'Edwardian Fair' scheduled for summer 1989: stalls, shows, lion tamer.

CERES

Fife Folk Museum

CRAIL

Crail Museum
64 Marketgate, Crail, Fife
(0333) 50869

Small local history museum with craft displays.

DUNFERMLINE

Dunfermline District Museum
Viewfield Terrace, Dunfermline
KY12 7HY   (0383) 721814

Local, social and natural history; emphasis on Dunfermline's linen industry in the 19th century.

Pittencrieff House Museum
Pittencrieff Park, Dunfermline
KY12 8QM   (0383) 722935/
721814

17th century mansion containing local social and municipal exhibits, costume and temporary art exhibitions.

INVERKEITHING

Inverkeithing Museum
The Friary, Inverkeithing KY11 1LS
(0383) 413344/721814

Small museum on Inverkeithing and Rosyth Dockyard; introduces Admiral Greig, putative founder of the Russian navy.

KIRKCALDY

Kirkcaldy Museum & Art Gallery

LEVEN

Leven Museum
Greig Institute, Forth Street, Leven
KY8 4PF   (0592) 260732

Museum above the library; photographs illustrating Leven as a Victorian and Edwardian resort.

NEWBURGH

Laing Museum
High Street, Newburgh KY14 6DX
(0337) 40223

Celebrates two Victorian scholars of Newburgh and shows their collections: geology, fossils, shells, Fijian ethnography.

ST ANDREWS

St Andrews Cathedral
St Andrews, Fife
(031) 244 3101/3087

Small museum at the now ruined cathedral displaying Celtic and medieval monuments, pottery and glass.

St Andrews Preservation Trust Museum
12 North Street, St Andrews, Fife (0334) 72152

In a reconstructed 17th century house; local history, with 19th century grocer's and chemist's shops.

GRAMPIAN REGION

ABERDEEN

Aberdeen Art Gallery

Aberdeen Maritime Museum

Anthropological Museum

Gordon Highlanders Regimental Museum
Viewfield Road, Aberdeen AB9 2LA (0224) 318174

Militaria and relics of the regiment, which was formed in 1794, including medals, uniforms, albums. Re-opening in 1990.

James Dun's House
Schoolhill, Aberdeen AB9 1FQ (0224) 646333

18th century town house with permanent displays and exhibitions arranged from Aberdeen Art Gallery.

Natural History Museum
Department of Zoology, University of Aberdeen, Tillydrone Avenue, Aberdeen AB9 2TN (0224) 40241 ext. 6413

Collection of invertebrates and vertebrates primarily for undergraduate teaching.

Provost Skene's House
Guestrow, off Broad Street, Aberdeen AB1 1AR (0224) 646333

17th century furnished house with displays of local history; painted ceiling of *c.*1630.

ALFORD

Grampian Transport Museum & Railway Museum

BANCHORY

Banchory Museum
Burgh Buildings, High Street, Banchory (0779) 77778

Small local history museum with items associated with Scott Skinner 'The Strathspey King'.

BANFF

Banff Museum
High Street, Banff (0779) 77778

Social history museum; astronomical instruments of James Ferguson; natural history collection of Thomas Edward.

BUCKIE

Buckie Maritime Museum & Peter Anson Gallery
Townhouse West, Cluny Place, Buckie AB5 1HB (0309) 73701

In the library; illustrates the history of the fishing town since 1800; Peter Anson water-colours.

BURGHEAD

Burghead Museum
16–18 Grant Street, Burghead, Moray IV30 2VE (0309) 73701

Displays on local history, geology and archaeology, including the Burghead bulls, carved Pictish stones.

DUFFTOWN

Dufftown Museum
The Tower, The Square, Dufftown AB5 4AD (0309) 73701

Housed with the Tourist Information Centre; illustrating the history of Dufftown and Mortlach Church.

ELGIN

Elgin Museum

FOCHABERS

Fochabers Folk Museum
High Street, Fochabers IV32 7EP (0343) 820362

In a former church; illustrating the history of the district; display of gigs and carts.

FORRES

Falconer Museum

HUNTLY

Brander Museum
The Square, Huntly, Aberdeenshire (0779) 77778

In the library; collection of local history including important archaeological finds.

INVERURIE

Carnegie Museum
Town Hall, The Square, Inverurie (0779) 77778

Local history including especially archaeological finds and Eskimo carvings; memorabilia from the old GNSR railway.

KEITH

Keith Museum
Church Street, Keith AB5 3BR (0309) 73701

Small display on the local history of the area.

LOSSIEMOUTH

Lossiemouth Fisheries & Community Museum
Pitgaveny Street, Lossiemouth, IV31 (0343) 813772

Collections on the fishing industry (the

'Zulu' boats originated here); reconstruction of Ramsay MacDonald's study.

MINTLAW

North East of Scotland Agricultural Heritage Centre

PETERHEAD

Arbuthnot Museum

PITMEDDEN

Museum of Farming Life
Pitmedden House, Ellon AB4 0PD
(065 13) 2352

Farmhouse and buildings (including a farmworkers' bothy) with important collection of farming implements.

STONEHAVEN

Tolbooth Museum
The Harbour, Stonehaven,
Kincardineshire   *(0779) 77778*

In the 16th century tolbooth; displays of local history

TOMINTOUL

Tomintoul Visitor Centre
The Square, Tomintoul AB3 9ET
(0309) 73701

Local history, with focus on peat cutting, climatology, geology, wildlife; a reconstructed farmhouse kitchen.

TURRIFF

Session Cottage Museum
Castle Hill, Turriff, Aberdeenshire
(0888) 63451

Mid-18th century 'but and ben' cottage with 19th century furnishings; temporary exhibitions on local history.

HIGHLAND REGION

AUCKENGILL

John Nicolson Museum
The Old School, Auckengill, Caithness
(0955) 3761 ext. 274

Opposite a broch site; concerns the archaeological history of Caithness, and John Nicholson, Auckengill antiquarian.

BETTYHILL

Strathnaver Museum
Clachan, Bettyhill by Thurso
KW14 7SQ   *(06412) 330*

In an old church; local history including the Strathnaver clearances; memorabilia of the Clan Mackay.

DINGWALL

Dingwall Museum
Town House, Dingwall, Ross-shire
(0349) 62116

Relics and mementoes of local history; military exhibits.

DUNBEATH

Dunbeath Preservation Trust
Portomin Road, Dunbeath
(05933) 233

Housed temporarily at Dunbeath Harbour; telling the story of the area.

Laidhay Croft Museum

FORT GEORGE

Fort George
Ardersier IV1 2TD
(031) 244 3101/3087

Infantry barracks still in use; period rooms give vivid account of 18th century conditions there.

Queen's Own Highlanders Regimental Museum
Fort George, Ardersier IV1 2TD
(0463) 224380

Extensive displays of history and campaigns since 1778; regimental trophies, uniforms and memorabilia.

FORT WILLIAM

The West Highland Museum

GAIRLOCH

Gairloch Heritage Museum

GLENCOE VILLAGE

Glencoe & North Lorn Folk Museum
Glencoe Village, Argyll

In two restored thatched cottages; local history including MacDonald and Jacobite relics; agricultural display.

GOLSPIE

Dunrobin Castle Museum

HELMSDALE

Timespan
Timespan Centre, Bridgend,
Helmsdale   *(04312) 327*

Lively reconstructions of scenes from the past in the Highlands; audio-visual programme.

INVERNESS

Inverness Museum & Art Gallery

KINGUSSIE

Highland Folk Museum

LATHERON

Clan Gunn Heritage Centre & Museum
Latheron KW5 6DL   *(05934) 302*
or (0955) 4771

Small museum concerning Clan Gunn and the history of Orkney and the North.

NAIRN

Nairn Fishertown Museum
Laing Hall, King Street, Nairn
IV12 4PD   (0667) 53331

Objects and photographs relating to the domestic life and fishing industry around the Moray Firth.

Nairn Literary Institute Museum

NEWTONMORE

Clan Macpherson House & Museum
Main Street, Newtonmore
PH20 1DE   (05403) 332

Displays tell the story of the clan; relics associated with Bonnie Prince Charlie.

ROSEMARKIE

Groam House Museum
High Street, Rosemarkie IV10 8UF
(0381) 20924

Small museum with carved stones, being reorganised (1988) as a Pictish centre for Ross & Cromarty.

ISLE OF SKYE

The Clan Donald Centre (Museum of the Isles)

Colbost Museum
Colbost, Isle of Skye   (047022) 208

A blackhouse furnished as in the 19th century; a reconstructed whisky still.

Luib Museum
Luib, Isle of Skye (047022) 208

A blackhouse showing living conditions in the early 20th century.

Skye Museum of Island Life

TAIN

Tain & District Museum & Clan Ross Centre

THURSO

Thurso Heritage Museum
Town Hall, High Street, Thurso
KW14 8AG   (0847) 62692

Concerning local history, especially the Caithness flagstone industry, Robert Dick naturalist and Sir John Sinclair.

ULLAPOOL

Lochbroom Highland Museum
Quay Street, Ullapool IV26 2UE
(0463) 2356

At the back of a bookshop; concerning Wester Ross – military, agricultural, social, and natural history.

WICK

Wick Heritage Museum

LOTHIAN REGION

ABERLADY

Myreton Motor Museum
Aberlady, East Lothian
(08757) 288

Bicycles, motorcycles, cars, charabancs, armoured vehicles, a few from 1900 or earlier.

BATHGATE

Bennie Museum
9–11 Mansefield Street, Bathgate, West Lothian

In two early cottages; local history, notably James Simpson, inventor of chloroform, and 'Paraffin' Young.

EDINBURGH

Camera Obscura
Outlook Tower, Castlehill, Royal Mile, Edinburgh EH1 2LZ
(031) 226 3709

In the Camera Obscura building;

displays of holography, pin-hole and space photography.

City Art Centre
2 Market Street, Edinburgh
EH1 1DE   (031) 225 2424
ext. 6650

Permanent collection of Scottish paintings and topography since 1800; principal speciality is important temporary exhibitions.

Cockburn Museum
Department of Geology, King's Buildings, West Mains Road, Edinburgh EH9 3JW
(031) 667 1081 ext. 3577

Large and important collection of rocks, fossils and minerals, geared mainly to undergraduate teaching.

Edinburgh Scout Museum
Edinburgh Scout Centre, 7 Valleyfield Street, Edinburgh EH3 9LP
(031) 229 3756

Illustrating nearly 80 years of scouting in Edinburgh and abroad.

Huntly House Museum

Lady Stair's House
Lady Stair's Close, Lawnmarket, Edinburgh EH1 2PA
(031) 225 2424 ext. 6593

In a house of 1622; relics and manuscripts of Burns, Scott and Robert Louis Stevenson.

Late Victorian Pharmacy
36 York Place, Edinburgh EH1 3HU
(031) 556 4386

Collection of historic pharmaceutical material displayed in a shop setting.

Lauriston Castle
Cramond Road South, Edinburgh
EH4 5QD   (031) 336 2060

The house of an Edwardian collector of 'objets d'art' preserved as it was in 1926.

Museum of Childhood

Museum of Communication
James Clark Maxwell Building,
University of Edinburgh, Mayfield
Road, Edinburgh EH9 3JL
(0506) 824507

Concerns mainly the history of
electrical communication from spark
transmitters to television.

Museum of Fire
Lothian & Borders Fire Brigade HQ,
Lauriston Place, Edinburgh
EH3 9DE   (031) 228 2401

Portrays the history of fire and the
Edinburgh Fire Brigade since 1600.

National Gallery of Scotland

The People's Story
Canongate Tolbooth, 163 Canongate,
Edinburgh EH8   (031) 225 2424
ext. 6638

Opening July 1989: reconstructions
and displays relating the lives, work
and pastimes of ordinary Edinburgh
people from the late 18th century to
the present day.

Royal College of Surgeons of
Edinburgh Historical Museum
Nicholson Street, Edinburgh
EH8 9DW   (031) 556 6206

Illustrating the history of surgery over
nearly five centuries, including Lister,
Dr Knox and others.

Royal Museum of Scotland, Chambers Street

Royal Museum of Scotland, Queen Street

Royal Observatory Visitor Centre
Blackford Hill, Edinburgh EH9 3HJ
(031) 667 3321

Display of telescopes, etc. and
explanations of modern developments
in astronomy addressed to the non-
specialist.

Royal Scots Regimental Museum
The Castle, Edinburgh EH1 2YT
(031) 336 1761 ext. 4265

Uniforms, medals and other
memorabilia of the oldest regular
infantry regiment in the British Army.

Scottish Agricultural Museum
Ingliston, Edinburgh
(031) 333 2674

A branch of the National Museums of
Scotland; displays on the social history
of Scotland's rural life.

Scottish National Gallery of Modern Art

Scottish National Portrait Gallery

Scottish United Services Museum

Talbot Rice Gallery
Old College, University of Edinburgh,
Edinburgh EH8 9LY
(031) 667 1011 ext. 4308

In the historic university quadrangle;
the Torrie collection of paintings and
sculpture; modern art exhibitions.

HADDINGTON

Jane Welsh Carlyle Museum
Lodge Street, Haddington EH41 3EE
(062082) 3738

Elegant 18th century house where Jane
Welsh lived and met Thomas Carlyle.

LIVINGSTON VILLAGE

Livingston Mill Farm & Countryside
Museum
Millfield, Livingston Village
EH54 7AR   (0506) 414957

18th century farm with working
watermill, children's farm and riverside
nature trail.

NEWTONGRANGE

Scottish Mining Museum (Newtongrange)

NORTH BERWICK

Museum of Flight
East Fortune Airfield, nr. North
Berwick, East Lothian
(031) 225 7534

A branch of the National Museums of
Scotland; interior and exterior displays
for the aircraft enthusiast.

North Berwick Museum
School Road, North Berwick
EH39 4JU   (0620) 3470

Local history including golf, natural
history and the history of the Royal
Burgh.

PRESTONPANS

Scottish Mining Museum
(Prestongrange)
Prestongrange, Prestonpans, East
Lothian   (031) 663 7519

See **Newtongrange**. The site of coal-
mining since *c.*1200; Cornish beam
engine; regular 'steam-up' days.

ORKNEY, SHETLAND, WESTERN ISLES

ORKNEY

Old Smiddy
St Margaret's Hope, Orkney KW17
(085 683) 366

Restored smithy; displays agricultural
machinery made by the smiths
themselves.

Orkney Farm & Folk Museum, Corrigall & Kirbuster

Pier Arts Centre, Stromness

Stromness Museum

Tankerness House Museum, Kirkwall

SHETLAND

Bod of Gremista (Booth of Gremista)
Lerwick, Shetland   (0595) 4632

Early 19th century booth connected with the fisheries; displays on Arthur Anderson, shipowner and philanthropist.

Haa of Tangwick
Hillswick, Shetland

Typical 18th century laird's house; displays of local interest.

Jarlshof
Jarlshof, near Sumburgh, Shetland
(031) 244 3101/3087

Visitor centre with explanations of this unusually complete archaeological site.

Old Haa
Burravoe, Yell, Shetland ZE2 9AY
(095 782) 339

Interpretative displays on past Shetland life.

Shetland Croft House Museum
Voe, Dunrossness, Shetland
(0595) 5057

Croft house, steading and mill furnished in late 19th century style.

Shetland Museum, Lerwick

Unst Heritage Centre
Haroldswick, Unst, Shetland
(095 781) 510/387

Displays on the island's social history, herring fishing, lace knitting and crofting.

ISLE OF LEWIS

Arnol Blackhouse

Museum Nan Eilean
Town Hall, Stornoway, Isle of Lewis
(0851) 3773 ext. 305

Concerns the history of Lewis and the town; including fisheries, domestic life, agriculture and archaeology.

Ness Historical Museum
Old School, Lionel, Port-of-ness, Isle of Lewis PA86 0TA   (085 181) 576

Artefacts, photographs, tapes, genealogies and videos relating to crofting and domestic life in Ness District.

South Uist Folk Museum
Bualadhubh, Eochar, South Uist PA81 5RQ   (08704) 331

Traditional thatched cottage of the outer Hebrides with appropriate furnishings; weaving loom and crofting tools.

STRATHCLYDE REGION

ALLOWAY

Burns Cottage & Museum

Burns Monument
Alloway, Ayr KA7 4PQ
(0292) 41321

Built 1823; contains memorabilia associated with Burns.

Maclaurin Art Gallery & Rozelle House

APPIN

Appin Wildlife Museum

Appin, Argyll PA38 4BN
(063 173) 308
Local wildlife specimens collected by the owner, for 22 years a ranger in Glencoe Forest.

AUCHINDRAIN

Auchindrain Open Air Museum of Country Life

BIGGAR

Biggar Gasworks
Gasworks Road, Biggar, Lanarkshire
(031) 225 7534

The old gasworks, built 1839; display of steam engines, gas lighting and appliances.

Gladstone Court Museum

Greenhill Covenanters' House
Burn Braes, Biggar ML12 6DT
(0899) 21050

Relates the story of the Covenanters 1603–1707 in a house of the period.

Moat Park Heritage Centre
North Back Road, Biggar ML12 6DT
(0899) 21050

The history and natural history of upper Clydesdale and Tweeddale from archaeology to acid rain.

BLANTYRE

David Livingstone Centre

BRODICK

Isle of Arran Heritage Museum
Brodick, Isle of Arran KA27 8DP
(0770) 22636

In old farm buildings; cottages, smithy, dairy and stables; local history, archaeology, geology and agriculture.

BUTE

Bute Museum
Stuart Street, Rothesay, Isle of Bute PA20 0EP   (0700) 2248

Local natural and social history; models of Clyde steamers, early Christian crosses, important archaeological section.

CAMPBELTOWN

Campbeltown Museum
Hall Street, Campbeltown, Argyll
(0586) 52366 ext. 218

In Victorian library building; local archaeological finds, natural history, fishing boat models.

COATBRIDGE

Summerlee Heritage Trust

ISLE OF CUMBRAE

Museum of the Cumbraes
Garrison House, Millport, Isle of Cumbrae KA28 0BG
(0475) 530741

Local history museum; displays on 19th century life and Bronze Age burial kist.

Robertson Museum & Aquarium
University Marine Biological Station, Millport, Isle of Cumbrae KA28 0EG
(0475 530) 581/582

In the oldest marine station in Britain; exhibits of fisheries and marine science.

DALMELLINGTON

Cathcartston Interpretation Centre
8–11 Cathcartston, Dalmellington, Ayr KA6 7QY　(0292) 550 426

A row of weavers' cottages of 1744; exhibits on the town's 18th century weaving industry.

DUMBARTON

Denny Ship Model Experiment Tank Building
Castle Street, Dumbarton
(0294) 78283

The first tank for testing ship models in a commercial shipyard, built 1883.

EASDALE ISLAND

Easdale Island Folk Museum

GIRVAN

McKechnie Institute
Dalrymple Street, Girvan, Ayrshire KA26 9AE　(0465) 3643

Local museum; exhibits include a Victorian cargo ship recovered off Argyll in 1977.

GLASGOW

The Burrell Collection

Glasgow Art Gallery & Museum

Hagg's Castle
100 St Andrews Drive, Glasgow G41 4RB　(041) 427 2725

History museum designed especially for children; regular children's craft workshops.

Hunterian Art Gallery

Hunterian Museum

Museum of Transport

People's Palace Museum

Pollok House
2060 Pollokshaws Road, Pollok Country Park, Glasgow G43 1AT
(041) 632 0274

Houses half the famous Stirling Maxwell collection of Spanish and other European art.

Provand's Lordship
3 Castle Street, Glasgow G4 0RB
(041) 552 8819

Built 1471, the only secular medieval building surviving in Glasgow; period rooms 1500–1918.

Royal Highland Fusiliers Regimental Museum
518 Sauchiehall Street, Glasgow G2 3LW　(041) 332 0961

Exhibits illustrate the story of the regiment from 1678.

Springburn Museum & Exhibition Centre
Atlas Square, Ayr Street, Springburn, Glasgow G21　(041) 557 1405

Items and continuous exhibitions on Springburn, formerly one of the world's principal locomotive works.

GREENOCK

McLean Museum & Art Gallery

HAMILTON

The Cameronians (Scottish Rifles) Regimental Museum
Mote Hill, off Muir Street, Hamilton ML3 8BJ　(0698) 428688

Exhibits illustrate the story of the regiment from 1689.

Hamilton District Museum
129 Muir Street, Hamilton ML3 6BJ　(0698) 283981

In old coaching house and assembly rooms; local history, especially transport and local topography.

IRVINE

Scottish Maritime Museum

ISLE OF ISLAY

Museum of Islay Life
Port Charlotte, Isle of Islay, Argyll PA48 7UA　(049 685) 358

Carved stones from the 6th century; local industry including distilling; Victorian displays include period rooms.

KILMARNOCK

Dean Castle

Dick Institute
Elmbank Avenue, Kilmarnock KA1 3BU　(0563) 26401 ext. 36

Important fossils, Scottish archaeological items, shells, small arms and ethnography; art gallery.

KIRKINTILLOCH

Barony Chambers Museum & Auld Kirk Museum
The Cross, Kirkintilloch, Glasgow G66 1AB (041) 775 1185

In an old town hall; social and industrial history of the Kirkintilloch district.

LARGS

Kirkgate House
Manse Court, Largs KA30 8AW (0475) 568 274

Exhibits relate to the Brisbane family, who lived here, having strong Australian connections; curling memorabilia.

Largs Monastery Museum
Benedictine Monastery, 5 Mackerston Place, Largs KA30 8DY (0475) 687320

(Formerly at Dumfries Priory.) On early Christianity and monastic houses in south-west Scotland.

MAUCHLINE

Burns House Museum
Castle Street, Mauchline, Ayrshire (0290) 50045

Artefacts belonging to Burns, who lived here; Mauchline box ware; display on local curling stones.

MILNGAVIE

Lillie Art Gallery
Station Road, Milngavie, Glasgow (041) 956 2351

Modern gallery mainly showing temporary exhibitions; small permanent collection of 20th century Scottish paintings.

PAISLEY

Coats Observatory
Oakshaw Street, Paisley, Renfrewshire (041) 889 3151

Built 1882; includes recent seismic equipment and satellite weather picture.

Paisley Museum & Art Gallery

RUTHERGLEN

Rutherglen Museum
King Street, Rutherglen, Glasgow G73 1DQ (041) 647 0837

History of the former Royal Burgh founded in the 12th century.

SALTCOATS

North Ayrshire Museum
Kirkgate, Manse Street, Saltcoats, Ayrshire (0294) 64174

In a former church; displays on local industries including lace and salt-making.

STRATHAVEN

John Hastie Museum
Threestanes Road, Strathaven ML10 6DX (0357) 21257

Local history, including the hand-weavers of Strathaven and covenanters; collection of pottery and porcelain.

ISLE OF TIREE

Skerryvore Museum
Hynish, Isle of Tiree, Argyll PA45 6UQ (08792) 691

Tells the story of building the Skerryvore Lighthouse.

TAYSIDE REGION

ALYTH

Alyth Museum
Commercial Street, Alyth, Perthshire (0738) 32488

Small museum with domestic and rural material from the area.

ARBROATH

Arbroath Art Gallery
Public Library, Hill Terrace, Arbroath, Angus (0674) 73232

Collection specialising in local work; water-colours by J.W. Herald.

Arbroath Museum
Signal Tower, Ladyloan, Arbroath, Angus (0241) 75598

Signal tower for Stevenson's 1813 Bell Rock Lighthouse; displays on the lighthouse, fishing, trades, wildlife.

St Vigeans Sculptured Stones
St Vigeans, near Arbroath, Angus (031) 2344 3101/3087

Pictish sculptured stones and medieval stonework from the original village church.

AUCHTERARDER

Strathallan Aero Park
Strathallan Airfield, nr Auchterarder PH3 1LA (07646) 2545

Exterior and interior display of aircraft, mostly from the World War II period.

BLAIR ATHOLL

Atholl Country Collection
The Old School, Blair Atholl, Perthshire PH18 5TT (079 681) 232

Local occupations – railway, post, kirk, school, smithy, gamekeeping, flax growing and spinning; children particularly encouraged.

Clan Donnachaidh (Robertson) Museum
Bruar Falls, Blair Atholl, Perthshire (079 683) 264

Documents, books and pictures associated with the history of the clan.

BRECHIN

Brechin Museum
St Ninian's Square, Brechin, Angus (0674) 73232

Local history including the Burgh Regalia, church plate, archaeology and trades.

COMRIE

Scottish Tartans Museum
Drummond Street, Comrie PH6 2DW   (0764) 70779

Comprehensive displays on the history of highland dress; reconstruction of a highland weaver's shed.

DUNDEE

Barrack Street Museum
Barrack Street, Dundee (0382) 23141

Scottish natural history; plans now ready to reorganise completely and transfer to Camperdown Wildlife Park.

Broughty Castle Museum
St Vincent Street, Broughty Ferry, Dundee   (0382) 23141

Reconstructed estuary fort; local history, especially Broughty Ferry itself, whaling and seashore life.

The Frigate 'Unicorn'
Victoria Dock, Dundee DD1 3JA (0382) 200900

Fifth-rate wooden frigate of 1824, the oldest British-built warship still afloat.

McManus Galleries

Mills Observatory
Balgay Park, Glamis Road, Dundee DD2 2UB   (0382) 67138

An active public observatory; small planetarium presenting slide shows; displays on astronomy and space exploration.

Royal Research Ship 'Discovery'

DUNKELD

Scottish Horse Museum
The Cross, Dunkeld, Perthshire

Tells the story of the Scottish Horse Yeomanry from 1900 to its amalgamation in 1956.

GLAMIS

Angus Folk Museum
Kirkwynd Cottages, Glamis, Forfar DD8 1RT   (030 784) 288

Displays of domestic and bothy life, period rooms and farm implements.

KINROSS

Kinross Museum
High Street, Kinross, Perthshire (0738) 32488

Small museum with items relating to Kinross and the neighbouring countryside.

MEIGLE

Meigle Sculptured Stones

MONTROSE

Montrose Museum & Art Gallery

William Lamb Memorial Studio
24 Market Street, Montrose (0674) 73232

The sculpture studio, workshop and livingroom of William Lamb (1893–1951); the artist's works and equipment.

PERTH

Black Watch Museum
RHQ The Black Watch, Balhousie Castle, Hay Street, Perth PH1 5HS (0738) 21281

History of the Black Watch Royal Highland Regiment since its founding in 1739.

Perth Museum & Art Gallery

WEEM

Castle Menzies
Weem, by Aberfeldy PH15 2JD (0887) 20982

In a 16th century castle undergoing restoration; artefacts associated with Clan Menzies.

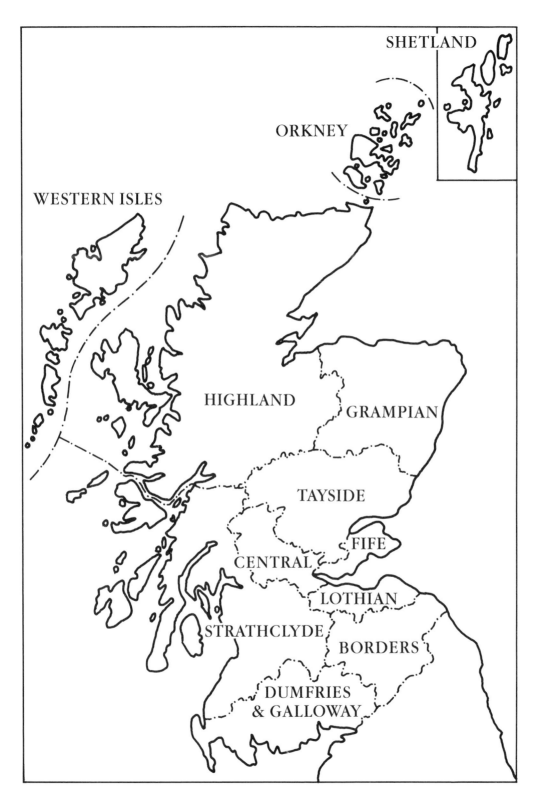

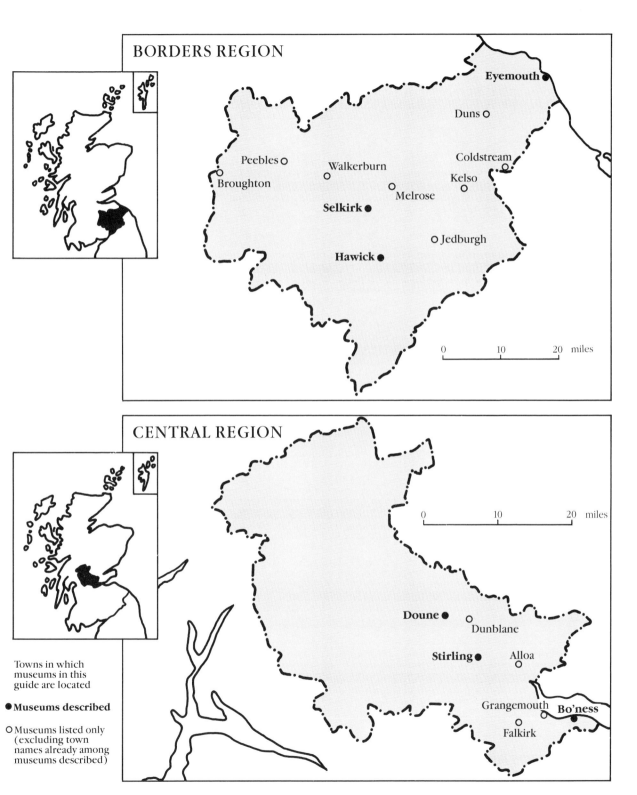

BORDERS REGION

Eyemouth

Duns ○

Peebles ○

Walkerburn

Coldstream

Broughton ○

Kelso ○

Melrose

Selkirk ●

Jedburgh ○

Hawick ●

0   10   20   miles

CENTRAL REGION

0   10   20   miles

Doune ●   ○ Dunblane

Stirling ●   Alloa ○

Grangemouth   **Bo'ness**

Falkirk

Towns in which
museums in this
guide are located

● **Museums described**

○ Museums listed only
(excluding town
names already among
museums described)

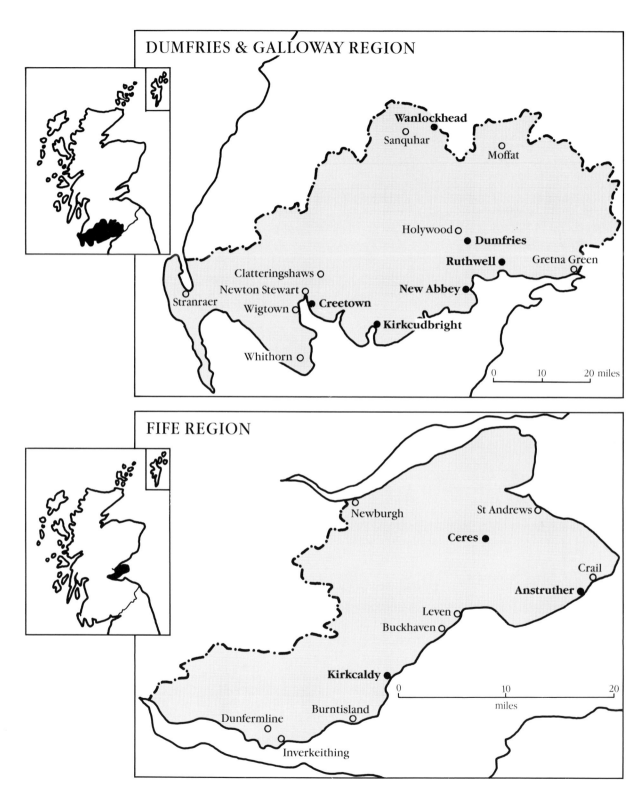

DUMFRIES & GALLOWAY REGION

Wanlockhead

Sanquhar

Moffat

Holywood

Dumfries

Ruthwell

Gretna Green

Clatteringshaws

Newton Stewart

Stranraer

Wigtown

Creetown

New Abbey

Kirkcudbright

Whithorn

0   10   20 miles

FIFE REGION

Newburgh

St Andrews

Ceres

Crail

Anstruther

Leven

Buckhaven

Kirkcaldy

0   10   20

miles

Burntisland

Dunfermline

Inverkeithing

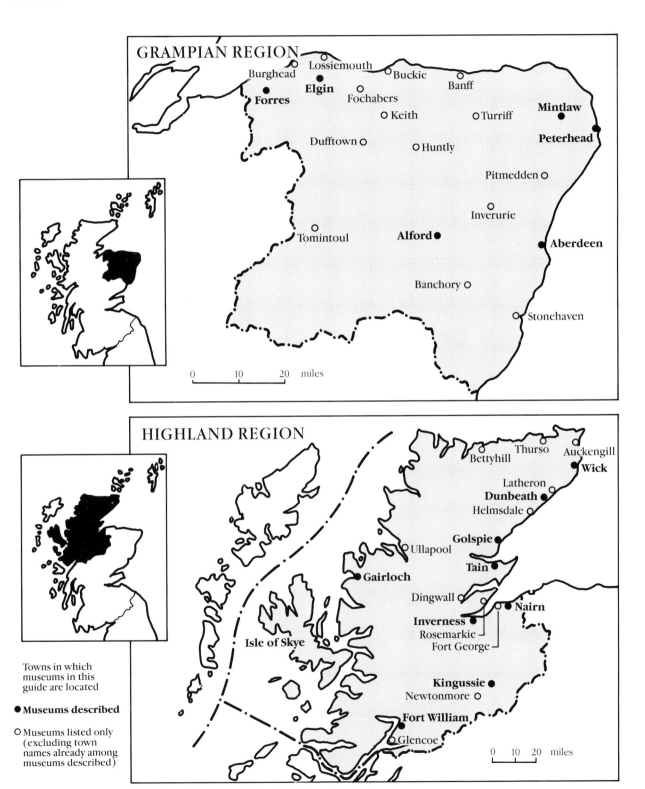

GRAMPIAN REGION

Lossiemouth
Burghead
Elgin
Forres
Buckie
Banff
Fochabers
Mintlaw
Keith
Turriff
Peterhead
Dufftown
Huntly
Pitmedden
Inverurie
Tomintoul
Alford
Aberdeen
Banchory
Stonehaven

0   10   20   miles

HIGHLAND REGION

Thurso
Auckengill
Bettyhill
Wick
Latheron
Dunbeath
Helmsdale
Golspie
Ullapool
Tain
Gairloch
Dingwall
Nairn
Inverness
Rosemarkie
Isle of Skye
Fort George
Kingussie
Newtonmore
Fort William
Glencoe

0   10   20   miles

Towns in which
museums in this
guide are located

● **Museums described**

○ Museums listed only
(excluding town
names already among
museums described)

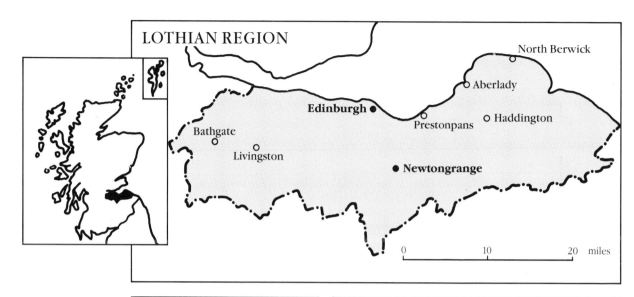

LOTHIAN REGION

North Berwick

Aberlady

Edinburgh

Prestonpans   Haddington

Bathgate

Livingston

Newtongrange

0   10   20   miles

ORKNEY ISLANDS

Corrigall
Stromness   **Kirkwall**

St Margaret's Hope

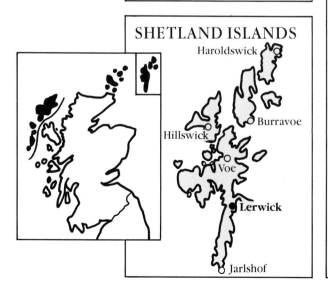

SHETLAND ISLANDS

Haroldswick

Burravoe

Hillswick

Voe

Lerwick

Jarlshof

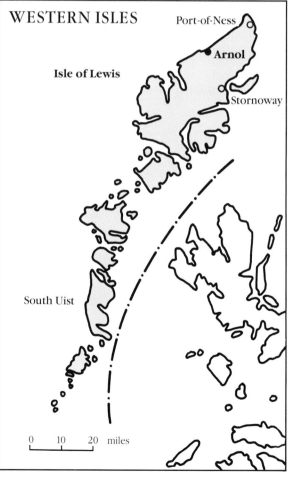

WESTERN ISLES

Port-of-Ness

Arnol

Isle of Lewis

Stornoway

South Uist

0   10   20   miles

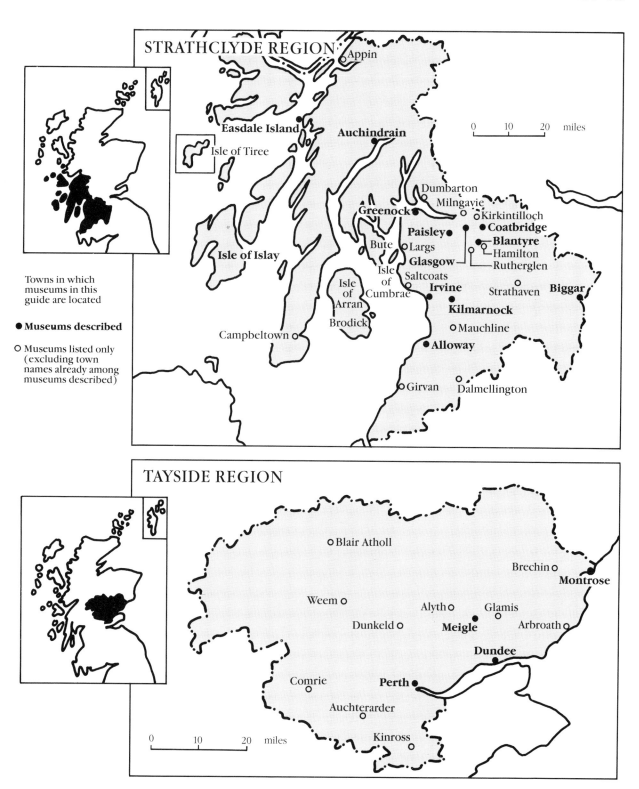

STRATHCLYDE REGION

Appin

Easdale Island

Isle of Tiree

Auchindrain

0   10   20   miles

Dumbarton
Milngavie
Greenock Kirkintilloch
Paisley **Coatbridge**
Blantyre
Bute Largs **Hamilton**
Glasgow Rutherglen
Isle of Islay Isle of Saltcoats
Cumbrae **Irvine** Strathaven **Biggar**
Isle **Kilmarnock**
of
Arran Mauchline
Brodick
Campbeltown **Alloway**

Girvan Dalmellington

Towns in which
museums in this
guide are located

● **Museums described**

○ Museums listed only
(excluding town
names already among
museums described)

TAYSIDE REGION

Blair Atholl

Brechin
Montrose

Weem Alyth Glamis
Dunkeld **Meigle** Arbroath

Dundee

Comrie **Perth**

Auchterarder

0   10   20   miles

Kinross

Index of Museum Names and Places

Printed in the United Kingdom
for Her Majesty's Stationery Office
Dd.240091 C50 7/90